SCIENCE

FOUNDATIONS

Reproduction and Cloning

SCIENCE FOUNDATIONS

Atomic Structure

The Big Bang

Biochemistry

Biodiversity and Food Chains

Cell Theory

Electricity and Magnetism

Evolution

The Expanding Universe

Forces of Nature

The Genetic Code

Germ Theory

Global Warming and Climate Change

Gravity

Heredity

Kingdoms of Life

Light and Sound

Matter and Energy

Natural Selection

Oceanography

Photosynthesis and Other Plant Life Processes

Planetary Motion

Plate Tectonics

Quantum Theory

Radioactivity

Reproduction and Cloning

Theory of Relativity

Vaccines

Viruses

The Water Cycle

SCIENCE
FOUNDATIONS

Reproduction and Cloning

PHILL JONES

CHELSEA HOUSE
An Infobase Learning Company

Science Foundations: Reproduction and Cloning

Copyright © 2012 by Infobase Learning

Chelsea House
An imprint of Infobase Learning
132 West 31st Street
New York, NY 10001

Library of Congress Cataloging-in-Publication Data
Jones, Phill.
  Reproduction and cloning / Phill Jones.
     p. cm. — (Science foundations)
  Includes bibliographical references and index.
  ISBN 978-1-61753-025-8 (hardcover)
  1. Reproduction—Juvenile literature. 2. Cloning—Juvenile literature. I. Title.
  QH471.J66 2012
  571.8—dc23   2011020003

Chelsea House books are available at special discounts when purchased in bulk quantities for businesses, associations, institutions, or sales promotions. Please call our Special Sales Department in New York at (212) 967-8800 or (800) 322-8755.

You can find Chelsea House on the World Wide Web at
http://www.infobaselearning.com

Text design by Kerry Casey
Cover design by Alicia Post
Composition by EJB Publishing Services
Cover printed by Yurchak Printing, Landisville, Pa.
Book printed and bound by Yurchak Printing, Landisville, Pa.
Date printed: November 2011
Printed in the United States of America

10 9 8 7 6 5 4 3 2 1

This book is printed on acid-free paper.

All links and Web addresses were checked and verified to be correct at the time of publication. Because of the dynamic nature of the Web, some addresses and links may have changed since publication and may no longer be valid.

Contents

Introduction to Reproduction

A basic trait of any living thing is the ability to reproduce. For thousands of years, philosophers and scientists mulled over the nature of reproduction and performed experiments to uncover the answers to two basic questions: Can a life form be created from nonliving material? What is the mechanism by which two living things produce offspring?

SPONTANEOUS GENERATION: MICE FROM UNDERWEAR

An uncovered piece of meat left outside appears to sprout maggots. A heap of garbage seems to give birth to mice and rats. These and other common observations once supported the ancient idea that some type of force that reorganizes nonliving matter to create life spontaneously exists. People clung to this belief in spontaneous generation, which is also called *abiogenesis*, for thousands of years. Over time, some scientists promoted an opposing view they called *biogenesis*: that living things arise only from other living things of the same type of organism.

Yet for many years, the notion of spontaneous generation captivated the minds of scientists. During the early seventeenth century,

Belgian chemist and physician Johann van Helmont wrote about his observations of the phenomenon:

> If you press a piece of underwear soiled with sweat together with some wheat in an open jar, after about 21 days the odor changes and the ferment, coming out of the underwear and penetrating through the husks of wheat, changes the wheat into mice. But what is more remarkable is that mice of both sexes emerge, and these mice successfully reproduce with mice born naturally from parents. . . . But what is even more remarkable is that the mice [that] come out [of] the wheat and underwear are not small mice, not even miniature adults or aborted mice, but [instead] adult mice emerge!

In 1668, Italian physician Francesco Redi performed an experiment to test the belief that rotting meat generates maggots. He placed pieces of meat in a number of containers, some of them open to the air, some of them sealed, and some with their openings covered with gauze. The rotting meat attracted flies. Soon, the meat in open containers sported a growth of maggots, but not the meat stored in closed containers. Flies that landed on gauze-covered containers laid eggs on the gauze. Maggots developed, even though they were not in contact with the meat. This indicated that the maggots did not arise from a vital force in the meat—they were simply the offspring of the flies.

Experiments by Redi and other scientists compelled supporters of spontaneous generation to admit that complex organisms did not arise by abiogenesis. Still, the existence of tiny organisms seen through microscopes invented in the mid-1600s, revitalized the popularity of spontaneous generation. Perhaps tiny life forms did arise by abiogenesis after all. Louis Joblot, a French mathematics professor, performed an experiment to test this idea by steeping dried hay in water to make an infusion. He then boiled the infusion to kill the microorganisms. Next, Joblot poured the liquid into two containers that had been heated to destroy any microbes. He sealed one container and left the other open to the air. Microorganisms grew in the open container, but not in the liquid of the closed one. Joblot concluded that spontaneous generation did not explain the growth of microbes in the open container: Microorganisms must have fallen into the container from the air.

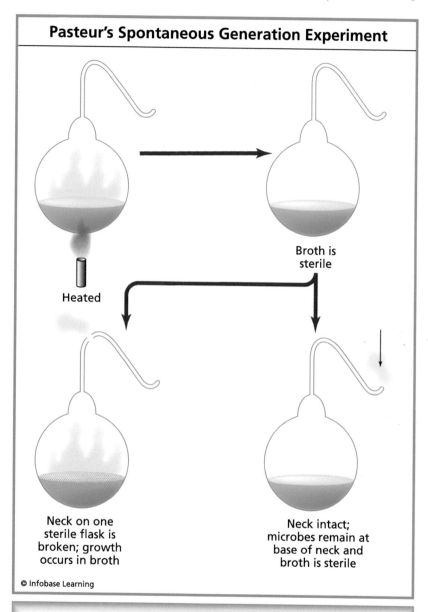

Pasteur's Spontaneous Generation Experiment

Heated

Broth is
sterile

Neck on one
sterile flask is
broken; growth
occurs in broth

Neck intact;
microbes remain at
base of neck and
broth is sterile

© Infobase Learning

Figure 1.1 Louis Pasteur used uniquely-designed swan-necked flasks
to dispel the theory of spontaneous generation.

However, despite Joblot's experiment, belief in spontaneous
generation persisted. Flawed experiments by other scientists continued to support the idea of abiogenesis until around 1860. That's

when French chemist Louis Pasteur put the debate to rest by showing that microbes traveling in air and dust could have contaminated experiments that appeared to support spontaneous generation. In one experiment, Pasteur poured meat broth into two glass flasks and then heated the necks of the flasks so that he could bend each neck into an S-shape. He reasoned that any microbes in the air would settle into the lower regions of the necks and not into the broth-filled bottoms of the flasks. Pasteur sterilized the flasks with heat and waited. The broth in both flasks remained sterile. After he tilted a flask so that the broth washed over the neck, the broth soon turned cloudy with the growth of microbes. "Never will the doctrine of spontaneous generation recover from the mortal blow of this simple experiment," Pasteur said during an 1864 lecture. "No, there is now no circumstance known in which it can be affirmed that microscopic beings came into the world without germs, without parents similar to themselves. Those who affirm it have been duped by illusions, by ill-conducted experiments, spoilt by errors that they either did not perceive or did not know how to avoid."

MICROSCOPIC HUMANS AND GENES

During the fourth century B.C., Greek philosopher Aristotle proposed that animals reproduce when a female's "inert fluid" mixes with a male's "vitalizing fluid." He also suggested that offspring develop in a gradual, stage-by-stage process similar to the way that a building is constructed from raw materials. William Harvey, who was physician for two English kings, elaborated on Aristotle's ideas during the early seventeenth century. Harvey proposed that an embryo builds its parts individually and according to a determined sequence. He called the process epigenesis. Harvey also proposed that the reproduction of humans and other mammals required a male fluid—semen—and a female's eggs. In Harvey's view, semen contributed nothing physical to the egg. Rather, semen provided a vital force that enabled an egg to become fertile and develop into an embryo. After energizing an egg, the semen simply dissolved or vaporized.

In the 1670s, Dutch linen merchant Antonie van Leeuwenhoek invented a single-lens microscope to examine cloth for flaws. He also used his invention to examine animal tissues. Other scientists soon peered through early, crude microscopes and thought that they saw

Figure 1.2 English physician William Harvey was the first person to make a detailed description of how blood is pumped through the body by the heart.

something remarkable: A human sperm cell harboring a miniature figure of a man. This apparent discovery suggested a preformation theory as an alternative to epigenesis. According to the preformation theory, a **gamete**—an egg cell or a sperm cell—contained a complete but miniature person, who enlarges during development. Supporters of the theory split into the spermatists, who believed that sperm cells held a preformed miniature human, and the ovists, who argued that it was the egg cells that contained a tiny person.

In 1759, German scientist Caspar Friedrich Wolff published his studies on the development of a chick embryo. He reported that

Testing Frog Sperm: Pants Required

In 1784, Italian priest and biologist Lazzaro Spallanzani performed a strange experiment. Among the many aspects of biology that interested him, Spallanzani was fascinated by the role of semen in frog reproduction. During normal breeding, male frogs clasp female frogs and deposit semen on the eggs as the female ejects the eggs from its body. To test the function of semen, Spallanzani needed a method for blocking its deposit on eggs. He recalled that another scientist had tried to clothe male frogs in pants to prevent semen from contacting egg cells. "The idea of breeches, however whimsical and ridiculous it may appear," Spallanzani wrote, "did not displease me, and I resolved to put it into practice." His experiment showed that eggs did not develop if the male frog wore trousers. After Spallanzani placed drops of frog semen on eggs, however, the eggs developed into offspring.

Spallanzani concluded that semen was required only to stimulate the fetal heart and promote growth of the life within the egg. However, his beliefs might have affected the way that he interpreted his observations. Spallanzani was an ovist; he believed in the preformation theory and chicken gametes do not contain preformed animals. Instead, layers of material develop into the body of the chick embryo. For example, an early chick embryo lacks heart and blood vessels; these tissues form as the embryo matures.

Scientists continued to uncover evidence that embryos develop in stages, which contradicted the preformation theory. Scientists also observed that male and female gametes combined to create an embryo, and that an egg cell and a sperm cell contained a spherical structure, which was named a **nucleus**. In 1876, German embryologist Oscar Hertwig studied the Mediterranean sea urchin, which produced

that the egg played the critical role in reproduction. He scoffed at those who argued that the male made the most important contribution to reproduction.

Figure 1.3 Lazzaro Spallanzani was so dedicated to aiding in discoveries about the body that he allowed his research colleagues to study his bladder after he died of bladder cancer in 1799. His bladder is now on display at a museum in Pavia, Italy.

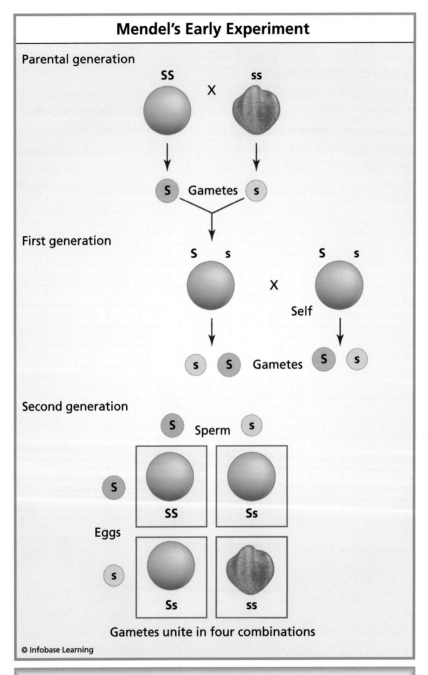

Mendel's Early Experiment

Parental generation

First generation

Second generation

Gametes unite in four combinations

© Infobase Learning

Figure 1.4   Gregor Mendel's experiments with pea plants helped him understand how traits are passed to offspring over generations.

transparent eggs ideal for microscopic examination. After mixing sea urchin egg cells and sperm cells, he saw a sperm cell entering an egg cell. The nuclei of egg and sperm cells fused into one nucleus.

At some point during the reproductive process, the characteristics of both parents must combine to produce traits seen in the new organism. During the nineteenth century, many scientists focused on another aspect of reproduction: How did the parents' characteristics transfer to offspring?

In 1856, Austrian monk Gregor Mendel began his experiments on heredity. During his eight-year study of the inheritance of seven traits in pea plants, he grew 28,000 plants. From his work, Mendel concluded that "form-building elements" (*bildungsfähigen Elemente*), or "units of inheritance," controlled the appearance of traits. These factors were inherited in pairs—one factor from the male parent and one factor from the female parent. Members of a pair of factors separate from each other during the formation of gametes. The combination of an egg cell and sperm cell produces a cell with a pair of the factors.

Here is another way to think about Mendel's conclusions. Consider the factor that causes a pea plant to sprout white flowers. The body cells of a pea plant contain two copies of these white flower factors, one copy inherited from each parent plant. During the formation of gametes, the pair of white flower factors separate. Both the egg cell and sperm cell contain only one copy of the white flower factor. An egg cell and a sperm cell fuse to form a cell that now has two copies of the white flower factor.

Mendel's formulation of the rules that govern the inheritance of traits was revolutionary. Yet his contribution to science went largely ignored. It took 30 years for other scientists to catch up with the monk.

During the late nineteenth century, German scientist Theodor Boveri, while studying the growth of sea urchin eggs, concluded that the nuclei of sperm cells and egg cells had the same amount of hereditary information. Compared with the nuclei of a sea urchin's body cells, the nuclei of egg cells and sperm cells contain half the number of rod-shaped **chromosomes**. After scientists rediscovered Mendel's work in 1900, Boveri realized that Mendel's factors shared similarities with chromosomes: Gametes had half the amount of chromosomes found in body cells. Other scientists

Cloning: Another Type of Reproduction

Unlike sexual reproduction, **asexual reproduction** does not require the fusion of egg cell and sperm cell nuclei. For example, certain animals, such as sea stars, can reproduce asexually when a fragment separates from the body and develops into a new animal. Offspring created by asexual reproduction are **clones**. That is, the offspring is a copy of the parent organism.

The concept of human clones thrives in science fiction. In response, the University of Utah's Genetic Science Learning Center warns about two common myths concerning human clones on its Web site. "Let's say you really wanted a clone to do your homework," the center asks. "[D]o you think this approach would really help you finish your homework . . . this decade?" No, cloning would not help, in the first place, because a clone would not begin its existence at the same age as the original. A clone would start as an embryo and age normally. A second myth about clones, the center warns, is that a clone will be a carbon copy of the original. "Are you familiar with the phrase 'nature versus nurture?'" the center asks. "Basically, this means that while genetics can help determine

studying reproduction in grasshoppers and fruit flies concluded that Mendel's factors, which were now called **genes,** are located in chromosomes within a nucleus. At the Rockefeller Institute in New York City in the 1940s, the experiments of Oswald Avery, Maclyn McCarthy, and Colin MacLeod proved that genes consist of **deoxyribonucleic acid (DNA)**.

THE RIDDLE OF SEXUAL REPRODUCTION

Sexual reproduction requires the fusion of egg cell and sperm cell nuclei. This simple statement is based upon the thoughts and traits, environmental influences have a considerable impact on shaping an individual's physical appearance and personality."

Even so, creators of science fiction movies often do not let facts get in the way of a story. Consequently, many films about human cloning include the Center's two myths. *The Island* (2005), for example, is set in the year 2019 and focuses on human clones who live in an isolated facility. The clones appear to arise both full grown and identical to their original human counterparts. As in several other films about human clones, scientists create human clones for the wealthy to supply custom-made, healthy spare organs. Science journalist Craig Cormick voices concerns about the effect of such grim science fiction movies on public perceptions.

> The negative depiction of cloning in films that play upon the worst stereotypes of evil and uncontrolled scientists fail to challenge us to think seriously about cloning, or consider the types of questions that would have to be considered if human reproductive cloning ever did become a reality. These include issues such as, what would be the rights of a clone? Who should decide who would be cloned? Or how might clones fit into society?

experiments of philosophers and scientists that took place over several thousand years. As new evidence accumulated, scientists settled the dispute between ovists and spermatists: Both sides were incorrect. An organism developed in stages from unformed tissues and did not wait in miniature for a time when it could expand into life. This basic understanding of sexual reproduction inspired new studies about heredity. Within a single century, scientists learned that "units of inheritance"—genes—controlled the appearance of traits, that genes are inherited in pairs, that a collection of genes from an egg cell and a sperm cell combine to produce an offspring's genes, that genes are located in chromosomes of cell nuclei, and that genes are made of DNA.

2

Processes Involved in Reproduction

The reproduction of any organism relies upon three types of molecules: deoxyribonucleic acid (DNA), **ribonucleic acid (RNA)**, and **protein**. DNA contains coded instructions that enable a cell to synthesize RNA molecules and proteins. Several types of RNA molecules play vital roles in the production of proteins, which are molecules that enable cells to perform activities necessary to sustain life.

FROM DNA TO PROTEINS

The Nature of DNA and RNA

Bacteria typically have a single, circular DNA molecule that contains the cell's genetic material. This DNA molecule is the organism's chromosome. Plant and animal cells have linear chromosomes arranged in pairs within the membrane-bound structure of the nucleus. The number of chromosomes contained within a nucleus varies among species. For example, a fruit fly cell has four pairs of chromosomes, whereas human cells have 23 pairs.

A DNA molecule is a **polymer**, which is a large chemical formed by combining smaller chemical units. The chemical units of a polymer are linked with each other by covalent bonds. A covalent bond is a strong form of chemical bond in which two atoms share electrons. In the case of DNA, covalent bonds link nucleotides. Each nucleotide has three parts: (1) a deoxyribose sugar molecule, which is a five-carbon sugar molecule called ribose that is missing a particular oxygen atom; (2) a phosphate molecule, which is a chemical group that contains phosphorus; and (3) a molecule called a **base**, which contains nitrogen.

The sugar group of one nucleotide binds with the phosphate group of another nucleotide to form a "sugar-phosphate-sugar-phosphate" structure, which is called the sugar-phosphate backbone of DNA. The bases of nucleotides stick out from the sugar-phosphate backbone. A DNA molecule has four types of bases—adenine, cytosine, guanine, and thymine—which are represented by the first letter of their names: A, C, G, and T. The base sequence "adenine-guanine-cytosine-thymine-guanine-adenine," for example, is represented by "AGCTGA."

Inside a cell, two single-stranded DNA molecules bind with each other to form a double-stranded helix. DNA molecules behave in this manner because certain bases are attracted to each other in a way that can be imagined as a type of magnetic attraction. The rules of attraction are simple: An A on one DNA strand of a double helix pairs with a T on the other DNA strand, and a G on one DNA strand pairs with a C on the other DNA strand. When bases of two different DNA strands bind together, they form a **base pair**. Consider a very short, double-stranded DNA molecule in which one strand has the following sequence: CATTAGCATGGACT. The other strand would have the sequence GTAATCGTACCTGA. Together, the strands would appear as follows:

CATTAGCATGGACT

GTAATCGTACCTGA

This is the case because the first C in **C**ATTAGCATGGACT pairs with the first G in **G**TAATCGTACCTGA, the first A in C**A**TTAG-CATGGACT pairs with the first T in G**T**AATCGTACCTGA, and so on. The base pairs, AT and GC, have the same overall shape. Since they have the same shape, an AT base pair and a GC base pair can fit into any order between the two sugar-phosphate backbones without deforming the helix.

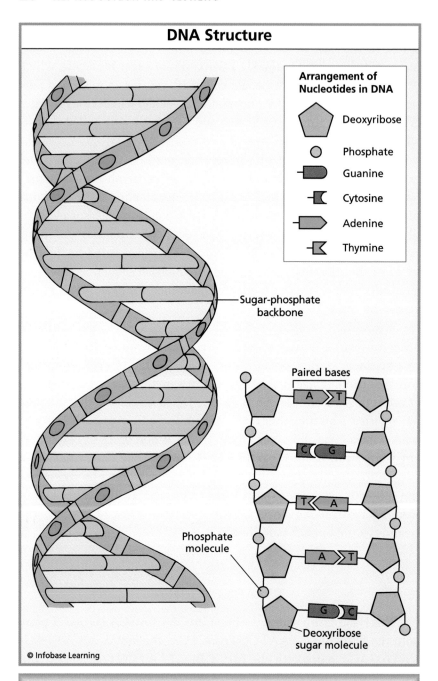

DNA Structure

Arrangement of Nucleotides in DNA

Deoxyribose

Phosphate

Guanine

Cytosine

Adenine

Thymine

Sugar-phosphate backbone

Paired bases

Phosphate molecule

Deoxyribose sugar molecule

© Infobase Learning

Figure 2.1 The structure of DNA resembles a ladder. The nucleotides twist in a double-helix, joined together by base pairs of nucleotides. The "rungs" of the "ladder" are made up of base pairs.

Like DNA, RNA is a polymer of nucleotides. However, RNA and DNA differ in three ways. First, RNA has a base called uracil that takes the place of thymine in DNA. For example, the sequence AGA TGT CCT in a piece of DNA would appear as AGA UGU CCU in an RNA molecule. A second difference between DNA and RNA is that DNA contains *deoxyribose* sugars, whereas RNA contains *ribose* sugars. A third difference is that RNA usually exists in the form of a single strand, whereas DNA can be found as a double-stranded helix.

Protein Synthesis

A DNA nucleotide sequence that provides the information a cell needs to synthesize a protein or an RNA molecule is a gene. **Gene expression** is the process in which a cell uses information stored in DNA to synthesize proteins and RNA molecules that affect the function or structure of a cell. To produce a protein, the data stored in DNA must be transferred to the cell's protein production machinery. In the process of protein synthesis, a protein polymer is formed by the addition of small molecules called amino acids that connect with each other by covalent bonds.

Two stages of protein synthesis are transcription and translation. During transcription, data is transferred from DNA by the synthesis of RNA molecules called *messenger RNA* (mRNA). Messenger RNA has a nucleotide sequence that is a copy of a nucleotide sequence found in a DNA molecule. (An mRNA molecule will not carry an exact copy of a DNA molecule's nucleotide sequence, because DNA uses thymine, whereas RNA uses uracil.) Messenger RNA molecules carry their recipes for a protein in the form of a **genetic code**.

The genetic code uses the four nucleotide bases found in RNA, organized into triplets of bases called *codons*. Triplets of four nucleotide bases provide 64 combinations (4 x 4 x 4). Since cells typically use 20 types of amino acids to synthesize a protein, 64 types of codons are more than sufficient to encode proteins. Some amino acids are encoded by 2 or more codons. For example, the amino acid leucine is encoded by the codons UUA, UUG, CUU, CUA, CUC, and CUG. Not all codons stand for an amino acid; some codons act as stop signals for protein synthesis.

translation, a cell's protein synthesis machinery translates codons in an mRNA molecule to produce a sequence of amino acids in a protein polymer. Translation depends upon molecules that ensure the assembly of the correct sequence of amino acids by binding an amino acid and its matching codon in mRNA. This critical function is performed by short, single-stranded RNAs that are called *transfer RNAs* (tRNAs). One end of a tRNA molecule has an anticodon—three nucleotides that can form base pairs with a codon in mRNA. At its other end, the tRNA carries an amino acid specified by the mRNA codon. A tRNA that carries its specified amino acid

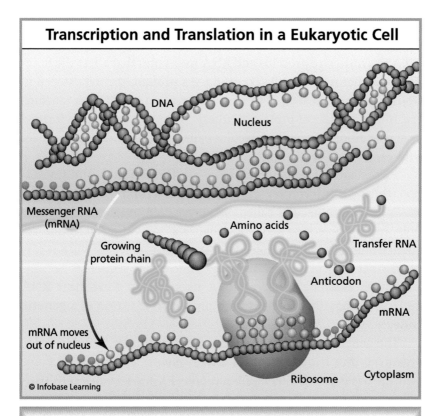

Transcription and Translation in a Eukaryotic Cell

DNA

Nucleus

Messenger RNA (mRNA)

Growing protein chain

Amino acids

Transfer RNA

Anticodon

mRNA

mRNA moves out of nucleus

Ribosome

Cytoplasm

© Infobase Learning

Figure 2.2 Transcription and translation are separate in eukaryotic cells. Transcription occurs in the nucleus to produce a pre-mRNA molecule. This molecule is typically processed to produce mature mRNA, which exists in the nucleus and is translated in the cytoplasm.

is often called a *charged tRNA*. Each tRNA can bind one specific type of amino acid. Therefore, a cell must contain at least one tRNA for each of the 20 common amino acids. Enzymes known as *tRNA transferases* recognize the unique features of a tRNA and attach the correct amino acid. These enzymes are the key to the transfer of genetic data in protein synthesis. They read the language of the genetic code found at one end of a tRNA and match the code to a specific amino acid.

An mRNA molecule and charged tRNAs meet at ribosomes, which are among the most complex structures within a cell. Ribosomes are composed of RNA and many proteins. The ribosomes of bacteria contain more than 50 different types of proteins, whereas human ribosomes have about 80 different proteins. A ribosome recognizes a signal in mRNA for the start of translation. Ribosomes also stabilize interactions between mRNA and charged tRNAs and supply enzymatic activity that links amino acids from the tRNAs to form a protein. As ribosomes move along an mRNA molecule, they expose the mRNA's codons one by one to ensure correct addition of amino acids. After ribosomes reach a stop codon, they detach from the new protein and the mRNA.

MITOSIS: CELL DIVISION THAT PRODUCES A CLONE

Scientists classify cells into a group of cells that have a nucleus and a group of cells that lack a nucleus. A *prokaryote*, such as a bacterial cell, is a one-celled organism that lacks a nucleus. A prokaryote can be divided into cytoplasm and a cell envelope. The cytoplasm is a gel-like matrix that fills the interior of the cell and contains DNA, RNA, proteins, and other important molecules. Most prokaryotes have a single molecule of DNA, which represents the cell's **genome**, the complete set of instructions for producing and maintaining the cell. The cell envelope of most prokaryotes consists of at least two parts: a plasma membrane and a cell wall. The plasma membrane encloses the cytoplasm and controls the types of molecules entering and leaving a cell. A rigid cell wall encloses the plasma membrane and imparts a shape to the cell.

A cell that has a nucleus is known as a eukaryotic cell. The outside of this cell is covered with a plasma membrane that retains the cell's contents, including a jelly-like mix of water and proteins called *cytosol*. A eukaryotic cell also contains organlike structures called *organelles* that perform vital functions. The nucleus, for example, is an organelle that stores **chromatin**, a mixture of DNA and proteins. Seen under the microscope, chromatin has a wiry, fuzzy appearance. When a cell is getting ready to reproduce itself, the chromatin compacts into the form of chromosomes. The cytoplasm also contains a cytoskeleton, which provides structure (like a skeleton) and movement (like muscles). The cytoskeleton is composed of long proteins,

Dawn of the Zombie Ants

From microscopic single cells to intestine-dwelling worms more than about 52 feet (16 meters) long, there are many forms of parasites. By living on or within one or more host organisms, parasites obtain nutrients and protection. Hosts also play vital roles in the reproduction of the parasite. For example, mosquitoes carry *Plasmodium* parasites, which are transferred with a mosquito's saliva when the insect bites a human. One type of *Plasmodium* invades human liver cells, reproduces, and then enters red blood cells and reproduces again, destroying the cells when they burst into the bloodstream. A mosquito that feeds on an infected human acquires parasites with its blood meal and transfers the parasites when it feeds on a healthy person.

Some parasites improve their chances of reproduction by controlling their hosts, turning the host organisms into mindless zombies. In 2009, researcher Dr. David P. Hughes of Harvard University described how a parasitic fungus manipulates the behavior of its ant hosts in a Thailand forest. After the fungus, *Ophiocordyceps unilateralis*, infects a carpenter ant, it forces the ant to leave its nest high above the forest ground to seek small plants. The zombie ant crawls onto the underside of the leaf of a plant which form tracks that allow molecules and cell components to move within a cell. The proteins also help to form extensions of the cell membrane that enable certain cells to travel.

Animals and other multicellular eukaryotes have two types of cells: **somatic cells** and gametes. In a multicellular eukaryote, the majority of cells are somatic cells. (The exceptions are egg cells and sperm cells, which are also called gametes.) A somatic cell reproduces itself by the process of **mitosis**, which is the division of a parent cell into new daughter cells. The nucleus of each daughter cell carries the same genetic information contained by the nucleus of the original, parent cell.

near the ground, and, just before the fungus kills it, the ant grabs hold of a leaf vein with its mandibles. The fungus grows inside the host, degrading the organs of the ant's corpse for nutrients. The muscles controlling the ant's mandibles and the insect's protective outer shell are left intact. The fungus produces a stalk that breaks through the back of the ant's head and eventually releases spores down to the forest floor, where prospective ant hosts may be crawling by.

Hughes' group found infected ants clinging with their death-grips to the undersides of low-hanging leaves located about 10 inches (25 centimeters) above the ground, an area that has optimal humidity and temperature conditions for fungus growth. "The fungus accurately manipulates the infected ants into dying where the parasite prefers to be, by making the ants travel a long way during the last hours of their lives," Hughes told reporters from LiveScience .com.

In 2010, Hughes announced that he and his team had been studying leaf fossils when they found evidence of the zombie ant death-grip in scars that were preserved in leaf fossils 48 million years old. So far, the fossils appear to provide the oldest evidence of parasites that can control the conduct of a host organism.

A eukaryotic cell lives through a cycle that begins with the production of daughter cells and ends when a new daughter cell completes its own process of division and produces its own two daughter cells. The cell cycle consists of four phases. The first, the Gap 1 (G1) phase, is the interval, or gap, between the creation of a new cell and DNA synthesis. During the second phase, the Synthesis (S) phase, the cell synthesizes proteins and DNA for copies of each chromosome. At the completion of the S phase, every DNA molecule has a duplicate. The Gap 2 (G2) phase, the third phase, is the interval between DNA synthesis and mitosis. Finally, the M phase begins with the division of the nucleus by mitosis and ends when the parent cell splits into two cells by cytokinesis.

The M phase, known as mitosis, deserves a close look. Mitosis proceeds through four stages:

1. *Prophase:* Long molecules of DNA compress into densely packed chromosomes. The membrane that surrounds the nucleus—the nuclear envelope—breaks down. Duplicate chromosomes are called sister chromatids, and they contain identical DNA molecules. Under the microscope, sister chromatids appear to have a waist at the point where they are most closely attached to each other.

2. *Metaphase:* Cytoskeletal protein cables attach to sister chromatids from two sides of the cell. The protein cables form a structure called the spindle apparatus. Spindle proteins pull chromatids to the cell's equator, which is called the metaphase plate.

3. *Anaphase:* Spindle proteins separate sister chromatids, pulling each member of a pair to opposite sides of the cell, so that each side has a copy of the cell's DNA. After separation, sister chromatids are called chromosomes.

4. *Telophase:* Chromosomes reach the two poles of the cell, and nuclear envelopes form, enclosing the chromosomes. Mitosis has ended.

During cytokinesis in an animal cell, a ring of proteins surrounds the cell and contracts, pulling like a drawstring. The contracting ring tightens the plasma membrane, and creates a furrow around the cell.

When the plasma membrane meets itself in the middle of the cell, it fuses and splits the old cell into two cells, each with its own nucleus and supply of cytoplasmic organelles. Cytokinesis proceeds differently in plant cells, which have a sturdy cell wall that surrounds the plasma membrane. In plant cells, a dividing cell assembles a new cell wall within the cell and between the two sets of chromosomes. As the new wall expands in two directions, it meets the parent cell's plasma membrane and cell wall, splitting the parent cell into two daughter cells.

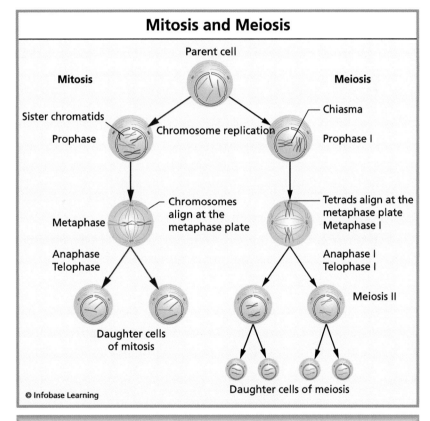

Mitosis and Meiosis

Parent cell

Mitosis

Meiosis

Sister chromatids

Chiasma

Prophase

Chromosome replication

Prophase I

Metaphase

Chromosomes align at the metaphase plate

Tetrads align at the metaphase plate
Metaphase I

Anaphase
Telophase

Anaphase I
Telophase I

Meiosis II

Daughter cells of mitosis

Daughter cells of meiosis

© Infobase Learning

Figure 2.3 Mitosis is a process that results in the formation of two new cells, each having the same number of chromosomes as the parent cells. Meiosis consists of two divisions (meiosis I and meiosis II) and results in four daughter cells, each containing the haploid number of chromosomes.

MEIOSIS: CELL DIVISION REQUIRED FOR SEXUAL REPRODUCTION

Eukaryotes multiply by sexual reproduction, using another type of cell division called **meiosis**. In many eukaryotes, cells divide by meiosis to form egg cells and sperm cells. Meiosis proceeds in two stages to create four daughter cells. The first stage of meiosis is similar to mitosis. The nuclear membrane breaks down, exposing the duplicated genome in the form of sister chromatids. Weblike proteins of the spindle apparatus attach to sister chromatids and pull them toward the middle of the cell. An important difference between mitosis and meiosis concerns the way that the spindle proteins divide genetic material into the two sides of the cell. In mitosis, each side of the cell receives a copy of the original genetic material. In the first stage of meiosis, spindle proteins do not divide chromatids into two identical sets.

As an example, suppose that a somatic cell contains only one type of chromosome, called chromosome 1. The cell would have two versions of the chromosome—one from the mother and one from the father. Call them chromosome 1m and chromosome 1f, respectively. The cell gets ready to divide, and its DNA duplicates. Now, the cell contains two copies of chromosome 1m and two copies of chromosome 1f. In mitosis, each side of the cell gets one copy of chromosome 1m and one copy of chromosome 1f. When the cell divides, the two daughter cells contain identical DNA. That is, each daughter cell has one copy of chromosome 1m *and* one copy of chromosome 1f. In the first stage of meiosis, each side of the cell gets two copies of chromosome 1m *or* two copies of chromosome 1f. When the cell divides, the daughter cells do not contain identical DNA.

During the second stage of meiosis, each daughter cell divides its set of chromosomes equally between two cells, so that each cell contains the same DNA. Each of the four daughter cells contains half the number of chromosomes of the original parent cell. In males, the four cells develop into sperm cells, while the cells develop into egg cells in females.

Scientists have divided the processes of meiosis into two stages, each with four steps.

Meiosis I

1. ***Prophase I:*** The nuclear membrane breaks down and the spindle apparatus forms. Structures of four chromatids can be seen under the microscope. A set of four chromatids consists of two sets of sister chromatids—one set inherited from the mother and one set from the father. For example, one group of four chromatids consists of two copies of maternal chromosome 1 and two copies of paternal chromosome 1. Arms from maternal and paternal chromatids overlap and fuse,

Chiasmata

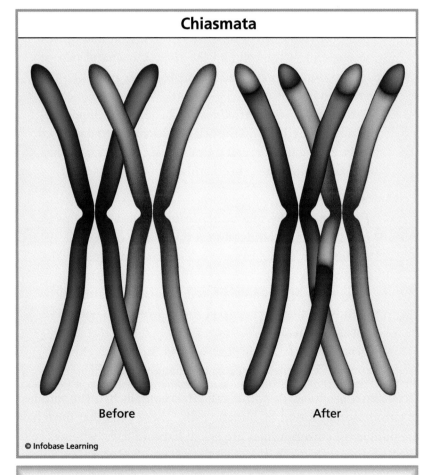

Before   After

© Infobase Learning

Figure 2.4   Chiasmata is the point of contact between paired chromatids during meiosis.

forming an X-shaped structure called a *chiasma* (plural: chiasmata).

2. *Metaphase I:* Spindle proteins pull sets of four chromatids—bound together by chiasmata—to the equator of the cell. At the end of metaphase I, the chiasmata disband, resulting in an exchange of genes between maternal and paternal chromatids. Chiasmata formation is one process that produces genetic diversity by creating new combinations of genes.

3. *Anaphase I:* Spindle proteins contract and separate maternal and paternal sister chromatids toward the two halves of the cell. For example, the sister chromatid pair of chromosome 1 inherited from the mother moves to one end of the cell and the sister chromatid pair of chromosome 1 inherited from the father moves to the other end of the cell.

4. *Telophase I and cytokinesis:* Nuclear envelopes enclose chromatids, and the cell divides into two daughter cells. Each daughter cell contains a set of chromosomes in the form of sister chromatids.

Meiosis II

1. *Prophase II:* The spindle apparatus forms and begins to pull sister chromatids toward the middle of the cell.

2. *Metaphase II:* Chromatids align at the equator the cell.

3. *Anaphase II:* Spindle proteins separate sister chromatids, so that each side of the cell receives one set of chromosomes.

4. *Telophase II:* Nuclear envelopes surround chromosomes. Cytokinesis creates two daughter cells.

Meiosis produces daughter cells that contain half the number of chromosomes found in somatic cells. These cells that have half the number of chromosomes are called **haploid** cells, whereas cells (such as somatic cells) that contain the full number of chromosomes are called **diploid** cells. Note that reducing the number of chromosomes is essential for sexual reproduction. If meiosis did not halve

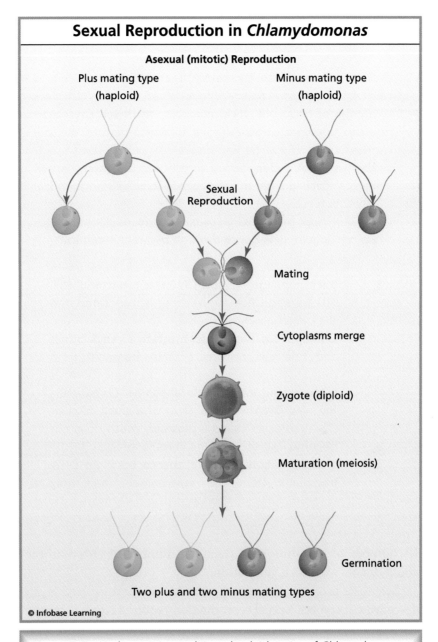

Figure 2.5 Under certain conditions, haploid strains of *Chlamydomonas* can unite to produce a diploid cell that can undergo meiosis to form four new haploid organisms. The two strains can also reproduce asexually when separate.

Reproduction of Bacterial Cells

Bacteria reproduce by *binary fission*, a process that is similar to mitosis. Before binary fission, a cell synthesizes a copy of its single DNA molecule, and each DNA molecule becomes attached to a different part of the cell membrane. When the cell divides by pulling itself apart, the two DNA molecules are distributed between the two halves. Each daughter cell typically contains an identical DNA molecule.

Although binary fission usually produces clones, bacteria can acquire new genes through several processes:

- Transduction: A virus that preys on bacteria—a bacteriophage—injects DNA into a bacterial cell. The foreign DNA can become incorporated into the bacteria's chromosome.
- Conjugation: Two bacteria attach to each other, and one cell obtains a DNA fragment from the other cell. Sometimes, the new DNA is incorporated into the chromosome. Sometimes, the new DNA is in the form of a small, circular DNA molecule called a **plasmid**, which does not become inserted into the chromosome.
- Transformation: Bacteria absorb bacterial DNA fragments from the environment and may

the number of chromosomes, then the number of chromosomes would double with each generation.

Scientists propose that sexual reproduction first evolved in single-celled eukaryotes. Sexual reproduction required two key components: the mechanism of meiosis and a means for cells of two different mating types to identify each other. Consider the freshwater green algae, *Chlamydomonas*, which is a single-celled, eukaryotic organism. Typically, a *Chlamydomonas* cell is haploid and contains just one copy of each of its 17 different chromosomes. A *Chlamydomonas* cell reproduces asexually by mitosis to produce two haploid daughter integrate the foreign DNA fragments into their chromosomes.

New genes can radically alter the characteristics of bacteria. For example, some plasmids carry genes encoding proteins that enable a bacterial cell to resist an antibiotic, such as an enzyme that destroys a drug. Currently, increasing numbers of drug-resistant bacteria pose a worldwide health problem.

The discovery of the transformation process highlighted a deadly consequence of gene exchange in bacteria. In 1928, Frederick Griffith, an English medical officer, studied the bacteria that caused pneumonia and found two forms of the microbe. One form (the R strain) had a rough surface and did not produce pneumonia, whereas another form (the S strain) had a smooth capsule that coated its exterior and caused the disease. Griffith killed deadly S strain bacteria by boiling them, and injected the heat-killed bacteria cells into mice. The mice survived. Then, he injected mice with a mixture of living R strain bacteria cells and heat-killed S strain cells. This time, the mice died. From the bodies of the dead mice, Griffith recovered living R strain cells and living S strain cells. By the process of transformation, living R strain cells had acquired DNA from the killed S strain cells, converting harmless R strain cells into deadly S strain cells.

cells, each containing the genes of the parent cell. *Chlamydomonas* reproduces sexually by using meiosis. Although this species does not have males and females, *Chlamydomonas* cells occur in plus mating type cells and minus mating type cells that engage in sexual reproduction. When a plus mating type cell contacts a minus mating type cell, proteins in the plasma membranes of the cells bind together. The cells merge into one cell and the two nuclei fuse into one nucleus. The fused cell is diploid, because the nucleus contains two copies of the 17 chromosomes—one set of chromosomes from each of the two mating types. After fusion, the process of meiosis begins.

Meiosis proceeds in two stages to create four haploid daughter cells. In the first stage, DNA duplicates to produce twice the number of chromosomes. At this point, the nucleus contains one pair of 17 chromosomes from the plus mating type cell and one pair of 17 chromosomes from the minus mating type cell. After the nuclear membrane breaks down, web-like proteins attach to chromosomes, and the proteins pull the chromosomes to two sides of the cell. Each side of the cell gets one pair of 17 chromosomes that are a mixture of chromosomes from the plus and minus mating type cells. The cell divides to produce two daughter cells. During the second stage of meiosis, each daughter cell divides its set of chromosome pairs equally between two cells, so that each cell contains the same DNA. The four daughter cells are haploid cells that contain a new arrangement of chromosomes.

ASEXUAL VS. SEXUAL REPRODUCTION

The reproductive process creates a new individual equipped with the necessary DNA-encoded instructions to synthesize RNA molecules and proteins that are required to sustain life. An organism can reproduce itself by asexual reproduction or sexual reproduction. In asexual reproduction, a new individual is created from the genes of one parent. The offspring is typically identical to the parent, and so is a clone of the parent. In contrast, sexual reproduction requires the combination of genes from two parents to create an individual with a unique arrangement of genes.

Asexual reproduction can enable cells to produce a large number of copies in a short time. Sexual reproduction requires more energy, time, and the coordination of cells from two different mating types. Yet, sexual reproduction offers a key advantage: Genes from two individuals combine into new arrangements. The ability to shuffle genes among members of a species was a significant development for life on Earth. Sexual reproduction enables a species to create genetic variation among its members. Genetic variation produces new combinations of characteristics in offspring. New characteristics may become critical for the survival of a species in a changing environment.

Animal Sexual Reproduction

The majority of an animal's cells are somatic cells, which have nuclei that contain a full set of chromosomes. In other words, somatic cells are diploid cells. Meiosis produces gametes that are haploid cells. In sexual reproduction, the nuclei of two haploid cells combine to produce a diploid cell, which is called a **zygote**. The zygote develops into a new individual.

In general, sexual reproduction requires two parents to supply two different types of gametes that merge to produce a zygote, which has genes from both parents. The female parent supplies gametes that are egg cells. Female animals typically produce small numbers of egg cells that may contain nutrients to support the early development of the zygote. The male parent supplies a large number of sperm cells, which are compact, mobile cells that deliver the male's genes to the egg cell. The process by which an egg cell and a sperm cell fuse to produce a zygote is called **fertilization**.

Sometimes, an animal produces both egg cells and sperm cells because it has both female and male reproductive organs. These animals are called hermaphrodites. Examples of hermaphrodites include earthworms, some snails, and some fish, such as certain Chinook salmon. Some hermaphrodites use their sperm cells to fertilize their own egg cells. The offspring are genetically identical to the parent and are, in effect, clones. However, hermaphrodites usually mate with another member of the same species to produce zygotes with a new combination of genes.

FERTILIZATION

The gametes that are produced by female and male animals are very different in structure and composition. These differences reflect the different functions of egg cells and sperm cells.

As an egg cell matures, it accumulates nutrients and other molecules that will be required by a zygote. For example, the egg cells of many animals store yolk proteins that will provide amino acids and energy for an early embryo. Since a young embryo synthesizes many proteins, an egg cell also stores tRNA molecules, ribosomes, and mRNAs. A sea urchin egg can store as many as 50,000 types of mRNA molecules and keep them ready for use by a developing embryo. As previously discussed, a plasma membrane encloses the cytoplasm of a cell. Depending upon the species, an egg cell can also include the vitelline envelope, which is a protective, fibrous mat that covers the plasma membrane.

The function of a sperm cell is to deliver a haploid nucleus to an egg cell. A sperm cell is a streamlined delivery system, and it does not need to store nutrients for an embryo. As a sperm cell matures, it loses most of its cytoplasm, which would otherwise be excess baggage. Its DNA compresses, enabling the sperm to have a compact nucleus. The nucleus resides in the "head" of a sperm cell. At the tip of a sperm cell is the acrosome, which contains a selection of enzymes. In most animals, the "tail" of a sperm cell is called a flagellum. This tail propels the sperm toward an egg cell. Long proteins within the flagellum convert chemical energy into mechanical energy that enables it to move.

When sperm cells contact an egg cell, proteins that cover the surface of the acrosome bind with proteins in the vitelline envelope of the egg cell. The binding between the proteins is specific, like the interaction between a lock and a key. Specific binding between sperm and egg cell proteins ensures fertilization of the egg cell with sperm of the same species. Enzymes from the acrosome degrade the vitelline layer. The plasma membrane of a single sperm fuses with the plasma membrane of the egg cell. Fusion activates a series of

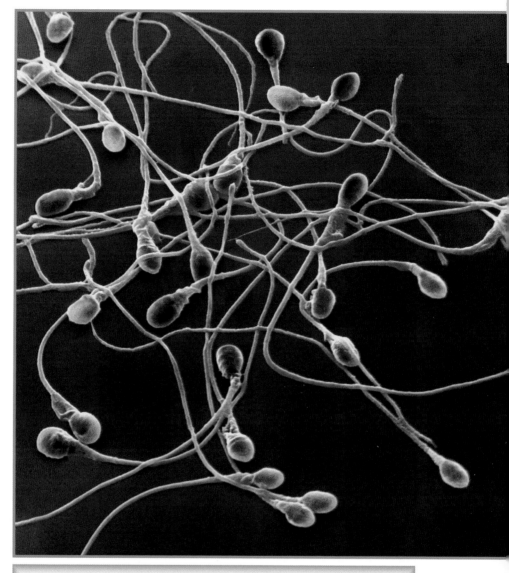

Figure 3.1 Human sperm cells move with the help of whiplike flagella.

reactions in the egg cell. In the egg cells of some animals, changes in the egg cell's plasma membrane block other sperm cells from fusing and entering the cell. This avoids the problem of multiple fertilization, which would result in a fertilized egg cell with too many sperm cell nuclei. Fusion of an egg cell nucleus with more than one sperm cell nucleus would create an abnormal number of chromosomes and a nonviable embryo. To prevent this lethal outcome, the egg cell also reacts to fusion with a sperm cell by secreting proteins to strengthen the vitelline layer into a barrier to other sperm. Egg cells of some animals, such as certain amphibians and birds, allow the penetration of more than one sperm cell. However, only one sperm cell nucleus fuses with the egg cell nucleus; all of the other sperm cell nuclei degrade.

Members of the animal kingdom produce fertilized egg cells by one of two methods: external fertilization and internal fertilization. Some animals deposit their egg cells and sperm cells in water. Sperm cells then swim through the water to the egg cells. Certain bony fish, for example, reproduce by releasing their gametes into the water. Although frogs live on land, most return to water to reproduce by external fertilization. Animals that live and reproduce on land use the process of internal fertilization. That means that the male deposits sperm inside the female, where sperm cells swim and fuse with

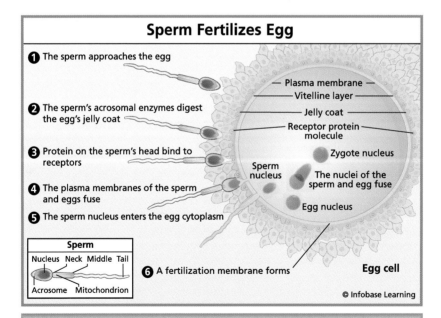

Figure 3.2   This illustration shows how sperm attaches to an egg and, ultimately, fuses with the egg's nucleus. A detailed diagram of sperm is shown in the inset.

egg cells. Some aquatic animals, such as sharks, also use internal fertilization.

OVERVIEW OF EMBRYONIC DEVELOPMENT

Early Development of an Embryo

Fertilization results in the production of a zygote with a diploid nucleus. A zygote divides by mitosis in a process called *cleavage*. First, the zygote divides into two daughter cells. Then, the daughter cells divide together to produce four identical cells, which divide to create eight cells, and so on. During development, mitosis continues to produce the many cells of the young animal.

In the early life of an embryo, cleavage in most animals produces a blastula, which is a multicellular embryo that typically has the form of a hollow ball of cells. A blastocoel is the fluid-filled cavity inside a blastula. During gastrulation, one end of the embryo folds inside the blastocoel to produce a pouch of cells that fill the cavity. In a gastrula, the outer layer of cells in the pouch becomes the ectoderm and the inner layer of cells becomes the endoderm. The outer covering of an animal develops from the ectoderm layer. In some animals, the central nervous system also develops from the ectoderm layer. The endoderm layer develops into the lining of the digestive tract, and in some animals, the endoderm layer also develops into the liver and other organs. Many animals produce three tissue layers as they mature: ectoderm, endoderm, and mesoderm. The mesoderm is a middle layer of cells that develops into muscles, as well as organs located between the digestive cavity and the outer covering.

The gastrula stage highlights an important point about embryonic development: Cell division alone is not sufficient to transform a zygote into a young animal. An embryo develops as cells **differentiate** from a general type of cell to a cell specialized to perform a specific function, such as the transfer of nerve impulses between various parts of the body. The process of altering the mass of cells of an early embryo into a shape that more closely resembles its parents is called *morphogenesis*.

(continues on page 42)

Asexual Reproduction of Animals

Asexual reproduction is reproduction that does not require the fusion of an egg cell nucleus and a sperm cell nucleus to produce a zygote with a new combination of genes. Instead, a parent creates an individual that often has identical DNA—a clone, in other words. Asexual reproduction is the method used by prokaryotes, such as bacteria, to reproduce. Although sexual reproduction is the primary method of animals, certain animals also can reproduce by asexual reproduction.

Fission is one method of asexual reproduction in the animal kingdom. An animal produces offspring by dividing itself in half, and each half develops into a mature animal. Sea anemones and flatworms can reproduce by fission.

Hydras are aquatic, solitary animals that have a cylindrical body and a feeding organ surrounded by tentacles. These animals can reproduce asexually by a process called budding. A new hydra begins life as an outgrowth from a parent. After it matures, the new hydra detaches itself from the parent. Although corals reproduce by budding, the new individuals remain attached to the parent to create a coral colony.

Certain worms, sponges, and sea stars can reproduce by the process of fragmentation and regeneration. In this process, one or more body pieces break from a parent organism and the fragments regrow missing parts until they develop into mature offspring.

In the process of parthenogenesis, an embryo develops from an egg cell without requiring the fusion of egg cell and sperm cell nuclei. In one form of parthenogenesis, an egg cell is formed by mitosis, not by meiosis. The offspring of ameiotic (meaning "without meiosis") parthenogenesis are clones of the parent. Another type of parthenogenesis, called meiotic parthenogenesis, occurs when a haploid egg cell is activated, even though a sperm cell nucleus has not fused with the egg cell nucleus. Chromosomal duplication can produce diploid cells of the developing embryo. In some forms of meiotic parthenogenesis, however, the progeny have haploid cells. Male honeybee drones are haploid animals that result from meiotic parthenogenesis.

Scientists have observed parthenogenesis in crustaceans, insects, fish, flatworms, Komodo dragons, sharks, and, in 2010, researchers discovered a female boa constrictor that reproduced by parthenogenesis. Mammals do not appear to reproduce by parthenogenesis. Nevertheless, Dr. Tomohiro Kono and colleagues at Tokyo University of Agriculture reported in 2004 that they had used technology to produce the first viable parthenogenetic mammal, a mouse named Kaguya.

Figure 3.3 A hydra buds in an asexual method of reproduction that results in clones.

(continued from page 39)

Just as a sculptor discards bits of clay that interfere with the shape of the sculpture, an embryo discards unnecessary cells and bits of tissue, This is achieved in a process called *apoptosis*, or programmed cell death. As a cell undergoing apoptosis shrinks, its DNA breaks apart, and pieces of the cell separate until the cell

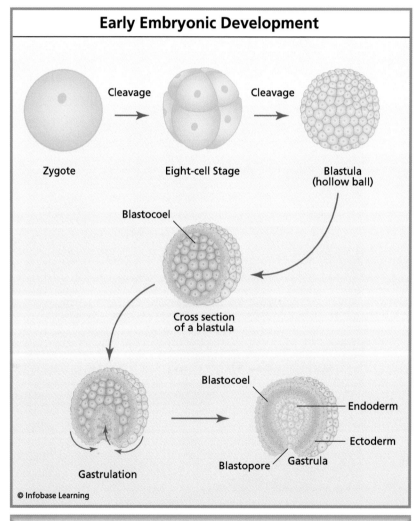

Early Embryonic Development

Cleavage

Cleavage

Zygote

Eight-cell Stage

Blastula
(hollow ball)

Blastocoel

Cross section
of a blastula

Blastocoel

Endoderm

Ectoderm

Gastrulation

Blastopore   Gastrula

© Infobase Learning

Figure 3.4 Early animal embryos go through a series of developmental stages.

disintegrates. Apoptosis plays a role, for example in the formation of chick and duck feet. Certain cells between the digits of a developing chick are programmed to die, whereas similar cells between the digits of developing ducks survive. As a result, ducks have webbed feet and chickens do not.

In sum, the transformation of a zygote into a young animal is achieved by mitosis to create new cells, differentiation to alter generalized cells to cells that have a specific function, and apoptosis to eliminate unnecessary cells. Normal development also requires the growth of some cells and the migration of certain cells to different parts of the body. All of these processes must take place in a coordinated manner to ensure survival of the individual and survival of the species.

Tactics for Protecting and Supporting Embryos

The extensive transformation that takes place during embryo development requires a constant source of nutrients. At the same time, the vulnerable embryo must be protected from predators and the environment. Animals use three basic strategies to meet these needs of their young:

* Most invertebrates (animals that lack backbones) and many vertebrates (animals that have backbones) are oviparous, meaning that they lay eggs. The embryos of oviparous animals develop in eggs exposed to the environment, which subjects the embryos to the risk of hungry predators. Desiccation can present another threat to eggs. Amphibians lay soft eggs coated with a jellylike membrane, suitable for wet environments where the risk of drying does not pose a problem. The hard-shelled egg of reptiles is an example of an adaptation to living on dry land. A reptile egg has compartments inside its protective shell, and each one has a different function for supporting the embryo. The chorion is a hard covering that prevents the loss of water, while it allows oxygen to diffuse inside the egg and waste carbon dioxide to diffuse from the egg. The allantois serves as storage for waste products of cell activity. The fluid-filled sac of the

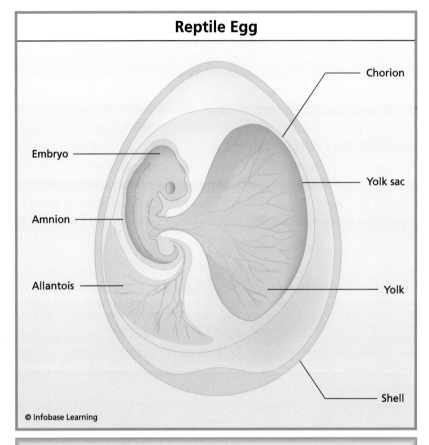

Reptile Egg

Chorion

Embryo

Yolk sac

Amnion

Allantois

Yolk

Shell

© Infobase Learning

Figure 3.5 An amniotic egg includes an amnion, which encloses the embryo in amniotic fluid for protection.

amnion protects the embryo and prevents dehydration. The yolk sac contains nutrients for the embryo.

- Earthworms, insects, and certain reptiles and fish are ovoviviparous animals. These kinds of animals store eggs within their bodies, and the developing embryos obtain nutrients from yolk stored in the egg.
- The embryos of viviparous animals obtain nutrients from the mother, and the young animal is born at an advanced stage of development. While certain amphibians, reptiles, fish, and scorpions are viviparous, most of the viviparous animals are mammals.

What do these three strategies suggest about fertilization? Egg-laying oviparous animals may fertilize egg cells internally or externally. However, fertilization must occur within a female's body in ovoviviparous and viviparous animals.

Sharks reproduce using internal fertilization. Depending upon the species, a shark can be oviparous, ovoviviparous, or viviparous. An oviparous shark, such as a horn shark, secretes a casing around an egg as it passes through the body. The casing produced by a horn shark is unusual: It has a spiral shape. A newly laid shark egg case is soft, but it quickly hardens to form a protective shell. Mako and sand tiger sharks number among the ovoviviparous sharks. The females produce eggs with thin membrane shells. Young embryos obtain nutrients from egg yolk or directly from the mother. In some species, a young embryo devours nearby eggs and embryos. Embryos of ovoviviparous sharks hatch within the mother and are released into the sea. The hammerhead shark is one of the viviparous sharks. Embryos obtain nutrients directly from the mother or from an organ called a yolk sac that absorbs nutrients produced by the mother.

Scientists have speculated that sharks played an important role in the evolution of internal fertilization among animals that have backbones. According to one theory, sharks and related aquatic animals first internally fertilized egg cells about 350 million years ago. However, in a January 2011 *Scientific American* article, John A. Long reveals evidence that internal fertilization and live birth first arose in a group of fish millions of years earlier.

In 2005, a team of scientists led by John A. Long, who was Head of Sciences for Australia's Museum Victoria, searched for fish fossils on a dry cattle ranch located in northwestern Australia. More than 300 million years ago, the land had been a reef covered by a shallow sea. The water had been populated with many forms of primitive fish, including armored fish called placoderms, an early backboned animal. One day, Long and his group discovered a 375 million year old fossil of a pregnant placoderm. The fossil contained an umbilical cord through which the female supplied nutrients to the developing embryo, evidence that the placoderms reproduced by internal fertilization and live birth.

Animals that reproduce by internal fertilization and give birth to live young produce fewer offspring than animals that reproduce by

(continues on page 48)

Metamorphosis

Many infant animals do not look at all like their parents. Instead, they exist as larvae, which often live in different environments than adult members of their species. The caterpillar larva of a moth, for example, crawls along the ground and on plants, while adult moths fly. Frog tadpoles must live in water, whereas adult frogs can live on land. A streamlined sea urchin larva travels on ocean currents, while mature, bulbous sea urchins usually stay in one place. The transformation of shape from such young animals to adult animals is called metamorphosis.

The majority of insects, including flies, bees, and butterflies, undergo metamorphosis with four stages:

1. **Egg:** This is the embryo stage of development.
2. **Larva:** After hatching from the egg, a larva eats and grows.
3. **Pupa:** A fully grown larva enters the pupa stage to transform its body, rearranging some organs and developing new ones. Typically covered with a hard case, the insect does not feed during this time. Many insects survive harsh winters in a pupa stage.
4. **Adult**: A developed adult breaks free of the pupa case, ready to reproduce and perpetuate the species.

The four-stage insect metamorphosis is known as complete metamorphosis. Grasshoppers, cockroaches and other insects develop through three stages of egg, nymph, and adult. In this "incomplete metamorphosis," the nymph eats and periodically sheds its skin to grow. After each skin shedding, or molting, the insect more closely resembles an adult insect until it reaches the adult stage.

Frogs are amphibians that undergo a radical metamorphosis. Frogs reproduce by externally fertilizing their eggs in water. After the gastrulation stage, a frog embryo begins to develop a tail. A tadpole—the frog's larval

(continues)

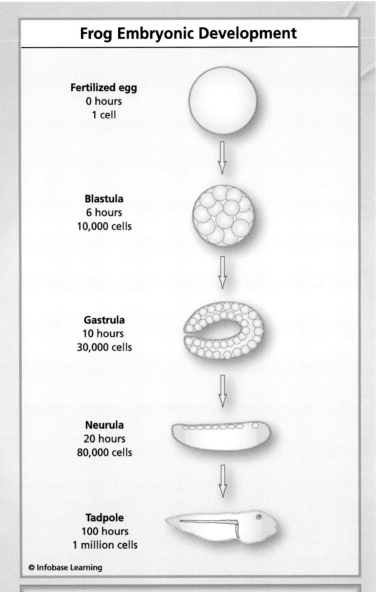

Frog Embryonic Development

Fertilized egg
0 hours
1 cell

Blastula
6 hours
10,000 cells

Gastrula
10 hours
30,000 cells

Neurula
20 hours
80,000 cells

Tadpole
100 hours
1 million cells

© Infobase Learning

Figure 3.6 In development of a frog embryo, the fertilized egg divides to produce a hollow ball of cells called a blastula, which changes form and folds to form a gastrula. But then the nervous system and a segmental spinal column develop, producing a neurula. A tadpole eventually forms into an adult frog after going through a stage called metamorphosis.

(continued)

stage—emerges from a protective coating, swimming through water with its tail and feeding on vegetation. During metamorphosis, the tadpole's tail and gills become absorbed into the body, while the animal develops forelimbs, hind limbs, and lungs for breathing air. The digestive system also changes. Although tadpoles are vegetarians, adults favor a carnivorous diet. Following metamorphosis, the young frog emerges from the water and climbs onto land.

(continued from page 45)

laying eggs for external fertilization. Nevertheless, John Long speculates that internal fertilization and live birth provided an advantage for placoderms. The key is that placoderms lived among numerous predators. Following a live birth, young placoderms would have been stronger and larger than the tiny hatchlings, wriggling from their eggs.

MAMMALIAN STRATEGIES

Mammals are a very diverse group of animals that occupy most habitats on the planet. Various features distinguish mammals from other animals, including mammary glands that produce nutrient-rich milk for the young, hair that serves as an insulator, and a large brain size. Most mammals share another characteristic: a fixed mating season. Depending upon the species, female fertility may be limited to a certain time during a periodic estrous cycle, and females copulate with males during a brief part of the cycle known as estrus. It is during estrus that egg cells become available for fertilization.

Mammals use three types of reproductive strategies. Scientists consider the oviparous, egg-laying monotremes—the duck-billed platypus and spiny anteater—to be the most primitive mammals. These animals live in New Guinea and Australia, and they produce eggs similar to bird eggs. A female platypus burrows into the ground to lay eggs, whereas the spiny anteater incubates eggs in a pouch. Unlike the mammary glands of other mammals, monotreme mammary glands lack nipples. A female secretes milk on her belly, and the young suck milk from the fur.

The group of viviparous marsupial mammals includes the kangaroo, opossum, and koala. After internal fertilization, a shell membrane forms around an embryo in the female's uterus. Several days later, the embryo breaks out of the shell and creates a depression in the wall of the uterus where the embryo absorbs nutrients with an organ called a yolk sac placenta. While still in an embryonic stage of development, a young marsupial crawls out of the mother's uterus and continues development outside her body. In most marsupial species, the young animal nestles into the mother's pouch and attaches itself to a teat as it continues to mature. Marsupials once lived around the world. Today, they live in the Australia region and in North and South America. North American marsupials are represented by a few species of opossum.

Ninety-four percent of living mammals are placental mammals, which are also viviparous. This group includes cats, bats, mice, wolves, whales, tigers, dogs, horses, apes, and humans. In a pregnant placental mammal, a **placenta** forms from the fusion of the lining of the mother's uterus and tissue from the embryo. A placenta enables the exchange of oxygen, nutrients, and a fetus' waste products between maternal blood and fetal blood. Placental mammals tend to spend more time caring for their newborn, compared with other animals.

A VARIETY OF SOLUTIONS TO THE CHALLENGE OF REPRODUCTION

Different animals achieve the union of a sperm cell and an egg cell by external fertilization or internal fertilization. After an egg and sperm cell fuse to create a zygote, the embryo undergoes complex and coordinated alterations to develop into a young animal. Cells rapidly divide, some cells differentiate to perform specific functions, and other cells die to sculpt organs and limbs into the proper form.

Depending upon the species, a developing embryo is protected by a hard shell or by the mother's tissues. The high energy demands of a developing embryo are met by nutrients stored within an egg, by nutrients supplied directly by the mother, or by nutrients supplied via a placenta, an organ created by the mother and the embryo.

Human Reproduction

L ike other placental mammals, humans reproduce by using the processes of internal fertilization and live birth. However, unlike any other life form on the planet, humans can devise treatments to overcome reproduction problems.

OVERVIEW OF HUMAN REPRODUCTION

From Gametogenesis to Ovulation

Gametogenesis is the production of gametes. In males, the process is called spermatogenesis. Within a testis, diploid cells called spermatogonia divide by mitosis to produce primary spermatocytes. By the process of meiosis, a diploid primary spermatocyte produces four haploid cells called spermatids, which mature into sperm cells. A mature sperm cell consists of three sections:

- a "head" that contains a haploid nucleus and at the tip of the head, an acrosome, which stores enzymes;
- a midsection that contains organelles called mitochondria, which generate chemical energy for the cell; and
- a tail, or flagellum, which propels the sperm cell toward an egg cell.

Adult males produce sperm continuously, hundreds of millions of them every day.

Human females create a limited number of egg cells. The production of egg cells, which is called oogenesis, begins within a female embryo's ovary. During this time, diploid cells (oogonia) divide by mitosis to produce diploid cells that are called primary oocytes. Primary oocytes start to divide by meiosis, but they stop at an early stage in the process. Scientists believe that the only primary oocytes that a human female will ever produce are the primary ones present in the ovaries at birth and halted in the meiosis process.

Protected within ovarian cavities called follicles, primary oocytes remain in the arrested stage until the age of puberty. Then, protein hormones from the brain travel in the bloodstream to the ovaries, where the hormones stimulate a group of follicles and their oocytes to continue development. A primary oocyte completes the first stage of meiosis to produce two cells: a secondary oocyte and a polar body. The polar body is a small cell with little cytoplasm; the cell eventually degenerates. The secondary oocyte stops development during the second stage of meiosis. During **ovulation,** a follicle breaks apart and releases a secondary oocyte. When a sperm cell penetrates this secondary oocyte, then the oocyte completes meiosis to produce a second polar body and a haploid egg cell. Like the first polar body, the second polar body has very little cytoplasm and is destined to degenerate.

Female gametogenesis and male gametogenesis are markedly different processes. Ovaries stop production of mature gametes after a woman has experienced about 500 cycles of ovulation (although it varies, this generally occurs when a woman is around 50 years old), whereas testes continue to produce sperm cells throughout a man's life. Spermatogenesis is a continuous process that produces four haploid gametes from one diploid cell, whereas oogenesis is a cyclic process with significant interruptions that produces one haploid gamete from one diploid cell. Cyclic ovulation is part of a complex menstrual cycle. Two components of the menstrual cycle are regulated by hormones: the ovarian cycle and the uterine cycle.

The Ovarian Cycle

At the beginning of a cycle, a hormone from one part of the brain (the hypothalamus) stimulates another part of the brain (the pituitary

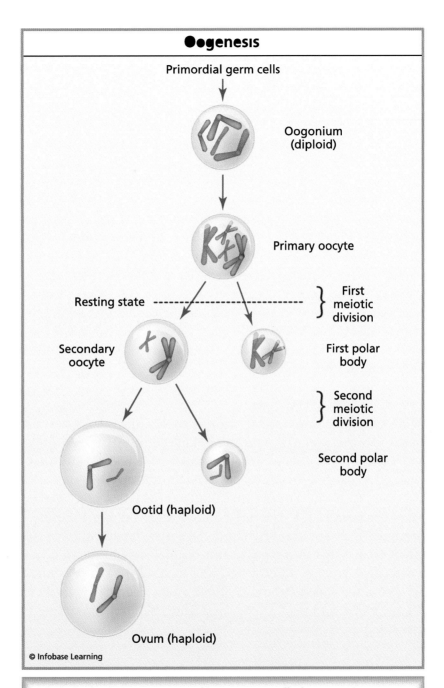

Oogenesis

Primordial germ cells

Oogonium (diploid)

Primary oocyte

Resting state --------------------------- } First meiotic division

Secondary oocyte

First polar body

} Second meiotic division

Second polar body

Ootid (haploid)

Ovum (haploid)

© Infobase Learning

Figure 4.1   An ovum is created in a process called oogenesis.

gland) to release two protein hormones into the bloodstream: FSH (follicle stimulating hormone) and LH (luteinizing hormone). When they reach the ovary, the two hormones stimulate growth of 3 to 30 follicles. As the follicles grow, they produce a hormone called estrogen, which travels in the bloodstream to the brain and stimulates the release of more FSH and LH. A sharp increase in LH release usually causes one mature follicle to rupture and release its secondary oocyte. The other maturing follicles degenerate, and the tissue of the burst follicle develops into gland-like tissue called a corpus luteum. Corpus luteum tissue secretes estrogen and progesterone hormones that cause the pituitary to reduce the release of FSH and LH. In turn, low levels of FSH and LH cause the corpus luteum to degenerate, and the tissue no longer produces its hormones. The decreased production of hormones from the corpus luteum allows the pituitary to secrete FSH and LH during a new cycle. Note that the corpus luteum serves an important function: It secretes hormones that inhibit the release of FSH and LH from the pituitary gland. Otherwise, a constant release of FSH and LH could stimulate the maturation of other follicles during pregnancy.

The Uterine Cycle

While ovarian follicles mature, they synthesize and release the hormone estrogen, which stimulates the lining of the uterus—called the endometrium—to thicken and to increase its blood supply. These changes prepare the endometrium to support the development of an embryo. The corpus luteum increases the production of progesterone, which causes the endometrium to further thicken and collect nutrients. If an egg is not fertilized, the corpus luteum degenerates after 14 days. After the corpus luteum disintegrates, ovaries produce a decreased amount of hormones, which causes the constriction of arteries in the endometrium. (Without a blood supply, tissue dies.) Tissue, blood, and fluid are released from the uterus, resulting in menstruation.

From Ovulation to Embryo Development

At ovulation, an ovary releases an egg cell into the abdominal cavity near the funnel-shaped opening of the fallopian tube, which connects with the uterus. Finger-like projections at the end of the fallopian tube move fluid into the tube enabling it to sweep an egg cell

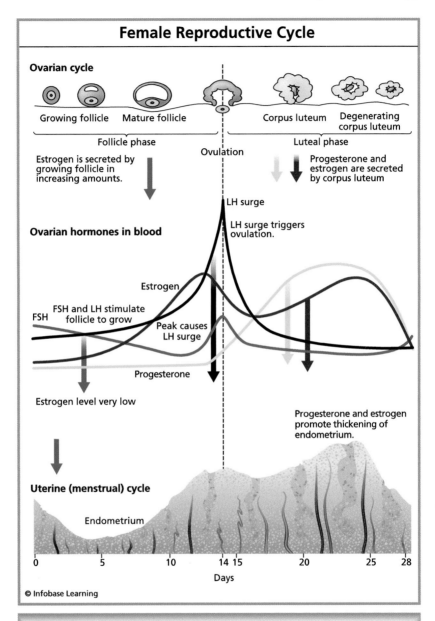

Figure 4.2 This illustration shows the female reproductive cycle, including changes in the ovaries, hormone levels, and uterine lining (endometrium) during a typical 28-day cycle. Day 1 is the start of the menstrual period. As the endometrium is shed, the pituitary gland releases follicle stimulating hormone (FSH) and luteinizing hormone (LH), which stimulate a new egg to mature in its follicle. At day 14, ovulation occurs and the body prepares for pregnancy. If the egg is not fertilized, estrogen and progesterone levels drop and the cycle begins again.

inside. The egg cell has about 12 hours to be fertilized. If fertilization (which is also called conception) does not occur, the egg cell degenerates.

For the egg cell to be fertilized, sperm released during sexual intercourse must swim through the vagina, into the uterus, and into the fallopian tube. A sperm cell that encounters an egg cell binds with the zona pellucida, a protective coating that covers the egg cell plasma membrane. Enzymes from the sperm cell's acrosome digest an opening and expose the plasma membrane of the egg cell. The sperm cell's outer membrane fuses with the egg cell's plasma membrane, and the haploid nucleus of the sperm enters the egg cell. The haploid nuclei of egg and sperm cells contain 23 chromosomes each. Fusion of the nuclei restores the number to 46 chromosomes—23 pairs of chromosomes—found in a diploid, somatic cell.

The fallopian tube is lined with small projections called cilia, which slowly shift the zygote to the uterus. The zygote divides by mitosis during this journey. Around five days after fertilization, the early embryo enters the uterus, and continues to divide to form a blastocyst, a hollow ball of cells. The blastocyst attaches to the endometrium in a process called **implantation**. By about nine to ten days, implantation is complete. The inner cells of the blastocyst continue to develop into the embryo, while some of the cells of the outer layer spread into the endometrium and help to form the placenta. The placenta anchors the embryo to the uterine wall and performs many other critical functions, such as the production of the hormone hCG (human chorionic gonadotropin). This hormone travels in the bloodstream to the ovary and maintains the life of the corpus luteum, which can continue to produce hormones that prevent ovulation. Note that hCG rescues the corpus luteum, which would otherwise degenerate and no longer produce hormones, resulting in menstruation. Eventually, hCG passes from the bloodstream and into the urine. Home pregnancy tests detect the presence of the hormone in urine.

The blastocyst wall develops into the chorion, a membrane that surrounds the embryo. An inner layer of membranes develops into the amniotic sac, which fills with a liquid that envelops the developing embryo. This amniotic fluid protects the embryo from physical injury.

sels begin to develop. By day 20, the heart is pumping fluid through the embryo's blood vessels. The blood vessels pass through the umbilical cord to the placenta. Here, oxygen and nutrients from the mother's blood diffuse into the embryo's bloodstream, while carbon dioxide and other waste products diffuse from the embryo and into the mother's blood. By about eight weeks after fertilization, basic forms of almost all of the organs have developed. At the end of the eighth week, the embryo is called a fetus. By about 23 to 24 weeks of pregnancy, the fetus may be sufficiently developed to enable it to survive outside of the uterus.

Human pregnancy is divided into three three-month stages called trimesters. During the first trimester (weeks 0 to 12), an egg

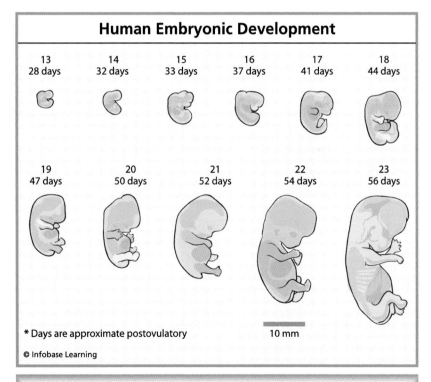

Figure 4.3   Selected stages in human development are shown. The first two weeks (not shown) are the preembryonic stage; weeks three through eight are the embryonic stage; and from eight weeks (56 days) onward is the fetal stage.

is fertilized, the embryo implants, and most organs form. During the second trimester (weeks 13 to 24), the placenta fully forms, and the fetus can respond to sound and grasp with its fingers. During the third trimester (weeks 25 to birth), the active fetus often shifts position, the lungs mature, and the head moves into place for delivery.

The development of a zygote into a fetus is a complex process that requires coordinated mitosis, differentiation of cells that perform specific functions, migration of cells from one part of the developing body to another, and programmed cell death, or apoptosis. Among other vital changes, apoptosis helps to ensure that the brain contains the proper spacing of nerve cells.

Talking About Regeneration

Some adult animals can regrow, or "regenerate," lost body parts. Certain insects, for example, can regenerate lost legs. Newts can regrow legs and tails. Like other mammals, humans cannot regenerate lost limbs or organs. However, humans can replace damaged organs by transplanting donated, functional organs, such as livers, lungs, hearts, and kidneys. According to the U.S. Organ Procurement and Transplantation Network, about 77 people receive an organ transplant every day in the United States.

The need for replacement organs and tissues exceeds the supply. Researchers strive to overcome this problem with laboratory-grown human tissue and organs, which can be transplanted into patients. The rat is a popular model for these studies in the field of regenerative medicine. In 2008, University of Minnesota scientists invented a technique to produce a beating rat heart in the laboratory, starting with fetal rat cells, blood vessels, and heart valves. Using lung cells from rat fetuses, Yale University scientists regenerated rat lungs in 2010. One barrier to human-sized organs is the need to ensure that the regenerated tissue has an adequate blood supply. "The inability to grow blood-vessel

INFERTILITY AND INFERTILITY TREATMENTS

Considering the many processes required for a successful pregnancy, it should not be surprising that some couples may face problems of **infertility**. Infertility is often defined as a failure to achieve pregnancy after at least one year of frequent sex without the use of contraception. An inability to achieve pregnancy can be caused by health problems of the man, the woman, or both partners. Most failures to become pregnant can be traced to three problem areas: sperm function, fallopian tube function, and the process of ovulation. Two

networks—or vasculature—in lab-grown tissues is the leading problem in regenerative medicine today," explained Dr. Jennifer L. West in a press release. "If you don't have blood supply, you cannot make a tissue structure that is thicker than a couple hundred microns [about 0.008 inch]." West, a professor of bioengineering at Rice University in Houston, Texas, announced in 2011 that she and her colleagues at Rice University and Houston-based Baylor College of Medicine had devised a way to grow blood vessels throughout a soft, plastic gel test system.

Other researchers are working on ways to repair damaged tissues within the body. During 2010, Professor Michael Schneider of Imperial College London reported that his research team invented a method for identifying rare cells in human hearts that can be stimulated to differentiate into heart muscle cells or cells that build blood vessels. The scientists plan to purify the cells in the laboratory, stimulate the cells to divide, and then transplant the cells into a patient to repair heart damage. Similarly useful cells can also be isolated from children's hearts according to Dr. Sunjay Kaushal, a surgeon at Children's Memorial Hospital in Chicago, Illinois. Kaushal plans to use heart cells to treat children born with damaged hearts.

common causes of male infertility are decreased sperm production and impaired sperm function. A male may produce inadequate numbers of sperm cells. A low sperm concentration is considered to be 10 million or fewer sperm per 0.034 ounce (1 milliliter) of semen. Even when sperm are produced in adequate numbers, the cells may have an abnormal shape or may lack the required motility to reach an egg cell.

A common cause of female infertility is a blockage or damage of the fallopian tube, the structure in which fertilization normally occurs. Impaired ovulation also causes infertility. Some ovulation disorders are caused by a decreased release of FSH and LH from the pituitary.

Sometimes, infertility can be treated with drugs. Protein hormones, such as human menopausal gonadotropin, can be injected to induce ovulation. Clomiphene is a drug taken orally that provokes the pituitary to release increased amounts of FSH and LH, which stimulate the maturation of ovarian follicles and cause ovulation. Clomiphene may also help men who have decreased sperm counts. The drug has this effect because FSH and LH stimulate and support the development of sperm in the testes.

A drawback to injectable fertility drugs is that they can stimulate multiple births by causing the ovulation of more than one follicle. The possibility of premature labor increases with a higher number of fetuses. An infant born prematurely faces an increased risk of health problems, including underdeveloped lungs and weak blood vessels in the brain.

Surgery may provide a solution for infertility. For example, a cluster of tangled blood vessels that drain the testes is a common cause of male infertility. Physicians propose that the tangled mass of blood vessels, which is called a varicocele, impair sperm production by increasing the temperature of the testes. Surgery can correct this condition. Surgery can also eliminate certain causes of female infertility, such as a blockage in a fallopian tube.

Assisted Reproduction Technology

During the 1950s, British scientist Robert G. Edwards thought that a method could be devised to help infertile couples by fertilizing egg cells and sperm cells under controlled conditions in a laboratory.

The zygote would be allowed to develop for a limited time in a culture dish and then, the early embryo would be transferred to the uterus of a future mother. Decades later, Edwards and clinician Patrick Steptoe invented the method of **in vitro fertilization** (IVF). In 1977, Lesley and John Brown visited Edwards' clinic seeking help; the Browns had failed to have a child after nine years of attempts. Doctors performed the new IVF technique, and on July 25, 1978, a healthy infant named Louise was born. Newspapers hailed her as the first "test tube baby."

Figure 4.4 Louise Brown and her parents, Lesley and John Brown, pose at home in Bristol, England. Louise made history as the first "test tube baby" when she was born in 1978.

IVF is very expensive, as well as physically and emotionally demanding on the woman. Nevertheless, couples seek IVF if they want a child who is biologically related to them, and also if simpler treatments have failed, such as infertility drugs, surgery, or artificial insemination, a procedure in which a physician transfers sperm directly to a fallopian tube for normal conception. The IVF process has five steps:

1. **Stimulation of ovulation**: To obtain eggs for fertilization, a physician administers fertility drugs to stimulate the maturation of ovarian follicles. This method is called superovulation, because multiple egg cells mature.

2. **Retrieval of egg cells**: A health care provider removes mature eggs from their follicles. Originally, a doctor performed this step by a inserting a tube-shaped instrument called a laparoscope. Today, a doctor removes egg cells with a hollow needle, guided by ultrasound examination. Ultrasound is a diagnostic technique that uses high-frequency sound waves to produce images of organs within the body. If the female partner has impaired ovaries, then a couple can obtain egg cells from an egg donor who may be either anonymous or known to the couple.

3. **In vitro fertilization**: Sperm donated by the male partner is mixed with egg cells. This step is called insemination. Sometimes, fertilization by insemination is not possible due to a problem with the male partner's sperm. In this situation, a technician may insert a sperm cell directly into an egg cell in a process called intracytoplasmic sperm injection. Some IVF clinics routinely perform this procedure to ensure fusion of egg and sperm cell nuclei. If sperm cannot be obtained from the male partner, then a couple may acquire the cells from a sperm donor.

4. **Culture of embryos**: Zygotes are maintained in culture dishes and allowed to grow for about five days. Pre-implantation genetic diagnosis may be performed during this time. The test can require the removal of one cell

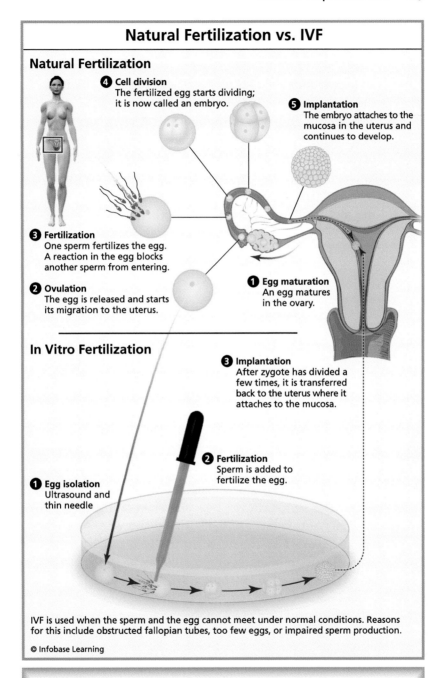

Natural Fertilization vs. IVF

Natural Fertilization

④ Cell division
The fertilized egg starts dividing;
it is now called an embryo.

⑤ Implantation
The embryo attaches to the
mucosa in the uterus and
continues to develop.

❸ Fertilization
One sperm fertilizes the egg.
A reaction in the egg blocks
another sperm from entering.

❷ Ovulation
The egg is released and starts
its migration to the uterus.

❶ Egg maturation
An egg matures
in the ovary.

In Vitro Fertilization

❸ Implantation
After zygote has divided a
few times, it is transferred
back to the uterus where it
attaches to the mucosa.

❷ Fertilization
Sperm is added to
fertilize the egg.

❶ Egg isolation
Ultrasound and
thin needle

IVF is used when the sperm and the egg cannot meet under normal conditions. Reasons
for this include obstructed fallopian tubes, too few eggs, or impaired sperm production.

© Infobase Learning

Figure 4.5 The stages in natural human fertilization and in vitro
fertilization, wherein sperm is fertilized outside the body, are compared.

from each eight-cell embryo. Scientists examine embryo DNA for the presence of genes associated with serious diseases. Pre-implantation genetic diagnosis provides an opportunity for a fertility specialist to select embryos that lack disease genes before implantation.

5. **Transfer of embryos to the mother:** A physician places embryos in the uterus. Typically, more than one embryo is transferred to increase the chances for embryo implantation and pregnancy. This practice can result in twins or triplets. Embryos that are not transferred to the mother may be frozen for another attempt in the

Who's Your Mama?

"What distinguishes surrogacy from other reproductive technologies is not the technology itself but the circumstances of its application—an arrangement whereby one woman bears a child for another, with the intent of relinquishing the infant at birth," wrote Sue A. Meinke, project researcher at the National Reference Center for Bioethics Literature at Georgetown University (Washington, D.C.). In one type of surrogate arrangement, a husband and wife contract with a woman—the surrogate—who will become pregnant by artificial insemination with the husband's sperm. The surrogate will bear the child and give up all parental rights in favor of the husband and wife. A couple typically seeks a surrogate when the wife cannot bear a child. This type of traditional surrogate arrangement received national attention during the Baby M trial.

In February 1985, Bill and Elizabeth Stern and Mary Beth Whitehead signed a surrogacy contract in New York, in which Whitehead agreed to artificial insemination with Bill Stern's sperm, and agreed to hand over the baby to the Sterns. However, Whitehead changed her mind after the birth of Melissa and fled to Florida with the baby. Police retrieved "Baby M," and Whitehead fought the surrogacy future. Frozen embryos may also be adopted by another couple. For more than 10 years, the Nightlight Christian Adoptions group has been running its Snowflakes Frozen Embryo Adoption & Donation Program to promote the adoption of donated frozen embryos by infertile couples.

Robert G. Edwards received the 2010 Nobel Prize in Physiology or Medicine for his work in the development of in vitro fertilization. According to the Nobel Foundation, IVF has enabled the birth of about 4 million people. During 2010, researchers at the Norwegian

contract in court. A judge enforced the contract. Whitehead appealed the decision to the New Jersey Supreme Court, which ruled in Whitehead's favor. The state supreme court decided that the surrogacy contract violated public policy, because the contract required the sale of a child. The media, politicians, religious groups, child welfare groups, feminists, and liberals condemned the practice of surrogacy on the grounds that it promoted baby selling, contributed to the exploitation of women, and affronted family values. State legislatures enacted laws to ban, or at least discourage, traditional surrogacy.

In 1993, the California Supreme Court decided in favor of a surrogacy agreement in *Calvert v. Johnson*. The case concerned a type of surrogacy arrangement in which a woman agreed to be a "gestational surrogate." The intended parents provided both egg and sperm cells, which were used to create an embryo by IVF. The embryo was then implanted in the gestational surrogate. The court decided that the intended mother—the egg donor—was the infant's legal mother based on the surrogacy contract. Following this decision, couples began to prefer gestational surrogacy, rather than traditional surrogacy. Today, some states do not enforce surrogacy contracts, while other states have legalized and regulate the practice of surrogacy.

University of Science and Technology in Trondheim published a series of reports showing that IVF does not affect the birthing process itself or the baby.

CONTROVERSIES ABOUT ASSISTED REPRODUCTION TECHNOLOGY

Various aspects of IVF have incited controversy, even before the process existed. During the 1970s, Edwards and Steptoe struggled against attacks on their work by the press and by colleagues. Religious leaders demanded an end to the research. Intimidated by senior scientists, some students refused to assist Edwards and Steptoe. Apparently concerned about global overpopulation, the government cut funding of the research; at that point, private donations stepped in to support IVF studies. "It has been an incredibly controversial research from the beginning," Nita Farahany, a philosophy professor at Vanderbilt University told *The Christian Science Monitor*. A member of the Presidential Commission for the Study of Bioethical Issues, Farahany says that, "Despite the incredible promises it offers, it's also raised significant bioethical issues that divide many people in society."

Perhaps the most controversial aspect of the IVF is the potential for its use to create customized babies. The practice of pre-implantation genetic testing sparks debate, because some people claim that couples could use genetic test results to select for cosmetic and physical traits of their children. Arthur Caplan, director of the Center for Bioethics at the University of Pennsylvania in Philadelphia, says that gene-altering technology also raises concerns. "I believe in the twenty-first century," Caplan told *The Washington Post*, "Edwards's discoveries will make the issue of designing our descendants—that is, trying to create children who are stronger, faster, live longer, that sort of thing—that's going to become the biggest issue in the first half of the twenty-first century."

Plant Reproduction and Cloning

According to scientific theory, plants evolved from ancestors of aquatic green algae and moved from water to land about 500 million years ago. Life on dry land offered increased access to sunlight and carbon dioxide for photosynthesis, a process that produces sugar molecules for chemical energy and for building cell components. Living on dry land also posed challenges that required plants to adapt to their new environment. Some plants evolved to reproduce asexually by spreading spores into the surroundings. A complex chemical covers spores to protect them from dry air. In another adaptation to life on land, a zygote develops into an embryo within the female parent's tissues, which protect the embryo and supply nutrients. Land-dwelling plants must obtain nutrients from the air and from the ground. Above the ground, plants obtain light energy and carbon dioxide, while soil provides minerals and water. In their search for nutrition, plants expand above and below the ground by growing from their apical meristems. Apical meristems are areas of active cell division found in roots and shoots. In most plants, shoot meristems produce leaves.

Most plants have a life cycle that varies between a generation with haploid (*n*) cells and a generation with diploid (*2n*) cells. A haploid plant is called a **gametophyte**, whereas a diploid plant is termed a **sporophyte**. Both gametophyte and sporophyte forms are multicellular. A plant alternates between the two forms, as shown in the following generalized plant life cycle:

Multicellular diploid sporophyte

↓

Sporophyte produces haploid spores
(within a sporangium) by meiosis

↓

Spores germinate and develop into
multicellular haploid gametophytes

↓

Gametophytes produce haploid gametes
(within gametangia) by mitosis

↓

Gametes fuse to form a diploid zygote

↓

Zygote develops into multicellular diploid sporophyte

Note that meiosis produces spores, not gametes. A diploid sporophyte uses meiosis to ensure that spore nuclei contain one copy of each chromosome (haploid), rather than two copies of each chromosome (diploid). Haploid spores develop into a haploid gametophyte. Since a gametophyte is haploid, it can produce haploid gametes by mitosis. Two haploid gametes fuse to form a diploid zygote. Although the haploid generation produces gametes, embryo development occurs in the diploid generation.

The plant kingdom encompasses a diverse group of life forms. Some plants have sporophyte and gametophyte phases that look so different that they appear to belong to different species. The dominance of the plant life cycle phase varies as well. A dominant phase is one that lives longer and may be larger than the non-dominant phase. In some plants, the gametophyte phase is dominant, while other plants have a dominant sporophyte phase. Some plants have a gametophyte phase that is microscopic. One evolutionary trend in plant development can be seen in a shift of the dominant phase. The more ancient plants have sporophytes that depend upon gameto-phytes for nutrients, whereas recently evolved plants have gameto-phytes that depend upon sporophytes.

Scientists have classified plants according to the presence or absence of a vascular system. Vascular plants have tubes that transport nutrients and water throughout the plant. The main parts of the vascular system are the xylem and phloem. In the xylem, narrow, hollow cells convey water and minerals from the roots to the plant body. The xylem can also help to support the plant body as it grows above ground. A tree's wood, for example, is composed of xylem. Phloem cells transport nutrients in the opposite direction. Most plants have leaves with cells that produce sugars by photosynthesis. The phloem carries sugars and other nutrients from the leaves to the rest of the plant body. In brief, vascular plants have a transport system that functions in two directions:

Water and → plant body ← sugars and other
minerals (roots)   nutrients (leaves)

The evolution of a vascular system allowed plants to grow taller, expanding above the surface where they could gather more energy from sunlight. Plants that lack a vascular system—the nonvascular plants—grow close to the ground.

REPRODUCTION OF NONVASCULAR PLANTS

The first plants to live on land were probably nonvascular plants called bryophytes. Because they lack a vascular system, bryophytes are small, usually reaching less than 5 inches (about 13 cm) in height. These plants can be found growing closely together in mats on the ground, logs, rocks, or trees. Instead of roots, bryophytes have delicate structures called rhizoids that anchor a plant to a surface. Rhizoids are slender strands of cells or tubular single cells. Lacking the vascular tissue of roots, rhizoids do not play a major role in the absorption of minerals and water from the soil.

The gametophyte phase dominates the life cycle of nonvascular plants. Compared with sporophytes, gametophytes live longer and are larger. Sporophytes may be invisible to the naked eye, attached to parent gametophytes to absorb water and nutrients from them.

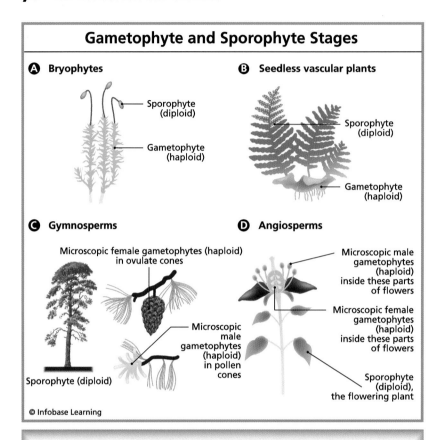

Gametophyte and Sporophyte Stages

Ⓐ Bryophytes

Sporophyte
(diploid)

Gametophyte
(haploid)

Ⓑ Seedless vascular plants

Sporophyte
(diploid)

Gametophyte
(haploid)

Ⓒ Gymnosperms

Microscopic female gametophytes (haploid)
in ovulate cones

Microscopic
male
gametophytes
(haploid)
in pollen
cones

Sporophyte (diploid)

Ⓓ Angiosperms

Microscopic male
gametophytes
(haploid)
inside these parts
of flowers

Microscopic female
gametophytes
(haploid)
inside these parts
of flowers

Sporophyte
(diploid),
the flowering plant

© Infobase Learning

Figure 5.1 The gametophyte stage is dominant in bryophytes, and the sporophyte is dependent on the gametophyte for nourishment. The sporophyte stage is dominant in seedless vascular plants, and the gametophyte is free-living. In gymnosperms, the gametophyte is reduced and is dependent on the sporophyte. In angiosperms, the gametophyte is also reduced and is dependent on the sporophyte.

Some bryophytes appear to lack a sporophyte phase. This type of bryophyte has gametophytes that can reproduce asexually: Plant fragments grow into new gametophytes.

With its 10,000 species, mosses have the greatest diversity among the bryophytes. These simple plants grow red-brown rhizoids, which anchor the moss, while their thin leaves absorb water and minerals. Mosses produce two types of spores that develop into male and female gametophytes. Male gametophytes produce sperm by mitosis, whereas female gametophytes use mitosis to produce egg cells. Water droplets enable sperm cells to travel to the female gametophyte where egg cells are produced. After fertilization, the sporophyte embryo develops within the female gametophyte, which also provides nutrition. Eventually, the sporophyte produces haploid female and male spores that germinate to create female and male gametophytes.

REPRODUCTION OF VASCULAR PLANTS

Most land plants are vascular plants, which are usually larger and more complex than nonvascular plants. The key trait of the vascular plants is a vascular system composed of xylem and phloem.

Figure 5.2 Green moss grows on a tree. Rhizoids are thin, rootlike structures that anchor the moss.

The roots of vascular plants anchor the plant, and play a vital role in transporting water and nutrients from the soil to the body of the plant. In addition to a vascular system and roots, most vascular plants have leaves that function as the main photosynthetic apparatus. Vascular plants also differ from nonvascular plants in their life cycles in that they have a dominant sporophyte phase.

The group of vascular plants is huge and can be divided into those that produce seeds and those that do not. The oldest type of vascular plant is the seedless plant.

Nonseed Vascular Plants

In ancient forests, ferns were the dominant plant life. Even now, they remain the most common seedless vascular plant. Most of a fern grows as an underground stem. The only part that appears above the surface is the series of divided leaves called fronds. A frond is also called a megaphyll, which means "large leaf," and this is one feature that distinguishes ferns from other seedless vascular plants. A frond consists of a leaf blade and a leaf stalk attached to an underground stem.

During the life cycle of a fern, diploid sporophyte plants produce haploid spores, usually on the underside of fronds. The spores are ejected from the fronds and are carried sometimes at great distances by the wind. Spores germinate and produce a small, heart-shaped gametophyte plant that is haploid and varies in thickness from one to several cells. The gametophyte produces egg cells and sperm cells. After traveling in water, sperm fertilize an egg cell and produce a diploid zygote. The zygote develops into an embryo that absorbs nutrients from the gametophyte. The gametophyte dies soon after the embryo has matured into a sporophyte. Unlike mosses, the sporophyte does not depend upon the gametophyte for nutrition: Both sporophyte and gametophyte phases of ferns can perform photosynthesis.

Ferns reproduce asexually, as well as sexually. In asexual reproduction, underground stems branch and grow a cluster of fronds above the surface. If the underground stem breaks, severing the connection between the frond cluster and the parent plant, then the frond cluster continues to grow as a separate plant.

Seed Vascular Plants

Around 360 million years ago, plants began to produce seeds. A seed consists of a plant embryo that carries its own supply of food to feed the embryo. Seeds are covered with a tough coat that shelters the embryo from environmental hazards. In contrast to spores of non-seed plants, seeds can remain inactive for years until conditions are favorable for germination. The last major evolutionary change in plant life arrived around 140 million years ago with the emergence of flowers that protect seeds and fruits that aid in seed dispersal.

Seed plants have the following traits:

* *Reduced gametophyte phase in the life cycle:* Unlike seedless plants, seed plants typically have gametophytes that are microscopic. The gametophytes are so small that they can be protected within the tissues of the sporophyte.
* *Heterospory:* Seed plants produce two types of spores: megaspores and microspores. Megaspores mature into female gametophytes, whereas microspores mature into male gametophytes. Female gametophytes produce egg cells, and male gametophytes produce sperm.
* *Pollen:* A grain of pollen contains a male gametophyte. Pollen grains are coated with a durable wall that protects the gametophyte. Seedless vascular plants and nonvascular plants produce sperm cells that must use flagella to swim in a layer of water to fertilize egg cells. This reflects methods used by ancient marine ancestors of plants. Pollen does not require water and can safely travel great distances.
* *Ovules:* An ovule is a structure that protects a megaspore, which matures into a female gametophyte that produces an egg cell. An opening in the protective coating of the ovule allows a pollen grain to enter. The pollen contains a male gametophyte that ejects sperm, which fertilize the egg cell. After fertilization, the ovule develops into a seed to protect the embryo.

Scientists divide the many seed plants into two groups: gymnosperms and angiosperms. Gymnosperms are nonflowering vascular seed plants, and angiosperms are flowering plants.

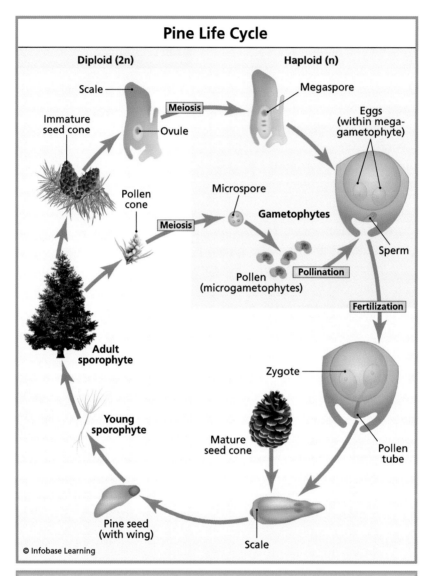

Pine Life Cycle

Figure 5.3   Pine trees have both ovulate and pollen cones. When a pollen grain has contact with an ovule, it germinates to form a pollen tube, inside which two sperm develop. Meanwhile, the female gametophyte undergoes meiosis, resulting in a single surviving megaspore. A female gametophyte in the megaspore forms several archegonia, each of which will form an egg. One sperm unites with each egg to form zygotes, which develop into the embryo within a seed. A new tree grows from the seedling.

Gymnosperms produce seeds on modified leaves. Typically, the leaves are arranged as cones. The gymnosperm group contains the longest-living and largest forms of life on the planet. Redwoods, pines, spruce, and ginkgos are examples of gymnosperms.

Consider the life cycle of pine trees. A pine tree is in a sporophyte phase with spore-producing sporangia that live on the scales of cones. Most types of pine trees have two kinds of cones: large ovulate cones and small pollen cones. Ovulate cones produce megaspores, which develop into female gametophytes. Pollen cones produce microspores, which develop into pollen containing male gametophytes. Carried by the wind, pollen grains land on an ovule, a step that is called pollination. A pollen grain forms a tube that digests tissue and moves toward the female gametophyte. As the tube extends, sperm cells develop in the tube, and the female gametophyte forms egg cells. More than one year after pollination, sperm cells fertilize egg cells. Seeds form and are dispersed by wind. With some types of pines, it takes about three years from the time that ovulate cones and pollen cones appear to the maturation of seeds for the next sporophyte generation.

Angiosperms produce seeds in an ovary, a structure that develops into a fruit. Flowering plants are the largest and most diverse group of plants, representing over 80% of the planet's green vegetation. The flower of an angiosperm is composed of modified leaves that form structures required for sexual reproduction. A flower is made up of the following basic components:

- Sepals that enclose a flower before it opens
- Petals that are interior to sepals and often have vibrant colors
- A carpel that contains an ovary, style, and stigma; the ovary, which has at least one ovule, sits at the base of the carpel; the style connects the ovary to the stigma, which receives pollen.
- A stamen composed of an anther and a filament that attaches an anther to the flower; pollen grains are produced in the anther.

The mature flower of a diploid sporophyte plant has anthers that form haploid microspores, which develop into pollen grains that

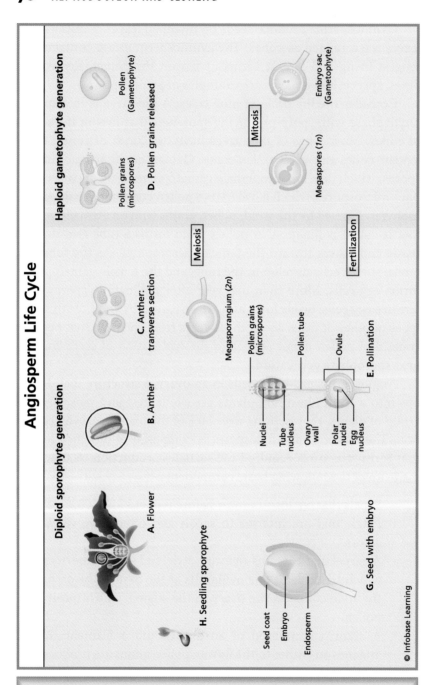

Figure 5.4   Angiosperms are the only group of plants with fully-developed flowers. They also produce specialized structures to support dispersal and germination of the seeds produced.

contain male gametophytes. A pollen grain has a generative cell and a tube cell. Female gametophytes develop within the ovules of an ovary and form egg cells. After pollination, a pollen grain forms a tube that extends to an ovule. The pollen grain generative cell produces two sperm. One of these sperm cells fuses with the egg cell, while the other sperm cell fuses with another cell within the ovule to form endosperm, a material that provides nutrients for the developing embryo. From there, a seed forms that contains an embryo along with its food supply. The wall of the ovary becomes thicker and matures into a fruit. Fruits protect the seeds and help to disperse them. Some fruits are eaten by animals. Protected by their tough coat, seeds pass through an animal and are excreted with fresh fertilizer. However, not all fruits are meant to be eaten. To boost dispersal by winds, the fruits of dandelions have feathery tufts that fly through the air like tiny parachutes, and those of maple trees have blades that

Figure 5.5 Aspen clones in fall colors, among other trees, cover Glacier National Park in Montana.

Self-fertilization or Cross-pollination?

One form of sexual reproduction in flowering plants is cross-pollination: Pollen from one plant travels to the stigma of a flower on another plant and fertilizes the plant's egg cells. For fertilization to occur, the pollen must reach a flower of the same species. Cross-pollination promotes the creation of a genetically diverse population, which increases the chance that at least one individual in a population can survive a changing environment.

Some flowering plants self-pollinate. This happens when the flower's sperm cells fertilize the flower's egg cells. Self-fertilization has advantages in areas that contain few pollinating insects or other flowering plants of the same species. The phenomenon in which self-fertilization ensures that seeds produce when pollinators or potential mates are scarce is called mating assurance.

Scientist Susan Mazer and her colleagues from the University of California, Santa Barbara discovered that seasonal drought may have exerted pressure for the evolution of self-fertilization among certain plants in the Evening Primrose family. The researchers studied four species of plants: Two species that are mainly self-fertilizers and two that are mainly cross-pollinators. The self-fertilizing plants had certain traits that resulted in a more rapid life cycle. These plants bloom weeks before cross-pollinating plants and before the beginning of the late spring

spin like those of a helicopter. Some fruits have barbs that attach to animal fur. After they land on new ground, the seed germinates into a young sporophyte.

Angiosperms also reproduce asexually to produce clones. In some plants, such as dandelions, a diploid cell in an ovule develops into an embryo, which becomes incorporated in a seed. This process does not require the fusion of egg cells and sperm cells. Another drought. The scientists suggested that the seasonal drought selected for the evolution of plants with a faster life cycle. Rapid flower development resulted in smaller flowers, which brought male and female sex organs closer together and increased chances for self-fertilization. By self-fertilizing, the plants avoid the most intense periods of drought.

However, self-fertilization also has disadvantages. Harmful mutations can accumulate in the flowering plants' genes. A **mutation** is a change in the nucleotide sequence of DNA that can alter proteins or RNA molecules encoded by the DNA. Another disadvantage of self-fertilization is that it creates a plant population that lacks genetic diversity.

A team of researchers led by two biologists from the University of Illinois at Chicago studied the nightshade plant family, which includes potatoes and other crop plants and has many species that cannot self-fertilize. "We've shown that a strong, short-term advantage experienced by individuals that have sex with themselves can be offset by long-term advantages to plant species that strictly avoid self-fertilization," assistant professor Boris Igic reported in a press release. "It's a trade-off," he said. "The short-term benefits of mating assurance and ability to invade a new environment are pitted against long-term advantages of greater genetic diversity, allowing plants that avoid self-fertilization to have more offspring during unpredictable environmental changes."

type of asexual reproduction—called fragmentation—occurs when a piece of a plant separates from the parent plant and then regenerates into a new plant. Some plants grow a runner, a slender stem that can grow along the ground. A runner sprouts new plants that are clones of the original plant. For instance, strawberry plants reproduce asexually by growing horizontal stems that produce new plants. Aspen trees can reproduce asexually from shoots that arise along lateral roots. Shoots develop into genetically identical trees that share a root structure. A group of such trees is called a clone and can cover 100 acres. For example, the Pando clone, located in the Fishlake National Forest in southern Utah, may be at least 80,000 years old and weighs more than 14 million pounds (more than 6.3 million kilograms).

CLONING PLANTS

Humans have used asexual reproduction of angiosperms to clone crop plants and flowers. A plant can be cloned from a fragment of the original plant, which is known as a cutting. Cuttings can be taken from stems, roots, shoots, or leaves. As one example, for more than 200 years, farmers have propagated Bartlett pears by asexual reproduction.

Most plant cells are **totipotent**, meaning that a complete plant can be grown from one plant cell. The property of totipotency makes it possible to clone plants from cells of an original plant. When incubated in a laboratory dish containing culture medium and certain plant hormones, plant cells can *de-differentiate*. This means that the cells change from cells with specialized functions, such as cells in roots, to cells with general functions. In culture, undifferentiated cells multiply and form a mass of generalized cells called a *callus*. Cells of a callus can be stimulated to differentiate into the many different cell types of the original plant by manipulating nutrients and plant hormones in culture medium. A callus can sprout roots and shoots and develop into a plantlet, which can be transferred to the ground. A callus can be divided into thousands of parts, which can be treated to develop into thousands of cloned plants.

Plant cloning by tissue culture has many applications. For example, orchid growers use cloning to produce thousands of identical plants from the root tips of a parent plant. Many types of African violet are produced by tissue culture cloning. An advantage of using this technique to grow flowering plants is that a group of genetically identical clones have the same stage of development and should flower at the same time, allowing a grower to market a large group of plants when they start to bloom.

The Downside to Cloning Yourself

Quaking aspen (*Populus tremuloides*) is the most widely-distributed native tree species in North America. Aspen grows across Canada, throughout the United States and into Mexico. The trees reproduce sexually with male and female flowers typically on separate trees. After fertilization, aspen produce small fruit that split and release tiny seeds that are spread by wind. The trees also reproduce asexually from shoots that develop along long, lateral roots. By this root sprouting, genetically identical clones share a common root system. A grove of aspens can consist of many groups of clones or one clone group.

Scientists suggest that some aspens have cloned themselves for up to a million years. Asexual reproduction spares aspen trees the chemical energy that is required to produce flowers and seeds, and the uncertainty that seeds will land in suitable ground for growth. Yet asexual reproduction has a cost. Researchers at Canada's University of British Columbia discovered that long-lived male aspen clones accumulate genetic defects. "The longer you clone yourself the more mutations you build up," biologist Dilara Ally told *Discovery News*. Ally and her colleagues analyzed accumulated mutations in the cells of more than 700 trees belonging to 20 different male aspen clones. They discovered that long-lived male aspen clones have mutations that reduce their ability to sexually reproduce by decreasing the amounts of viable pollen. If male aspen clones cannot reproduce sexually, then female trees cannot produce seeds ready for wind dispersal. The aspen clones cannot spread beyond their local environment.

Scientists use plant tissue culture cloning to ensure the survival of certain plants, such as England's famous Bramley apple. In 1809, a young girl named Mary Ann Brailsford planted apple seeds in pots. After the seeds germinated, she replanted them in her cottage

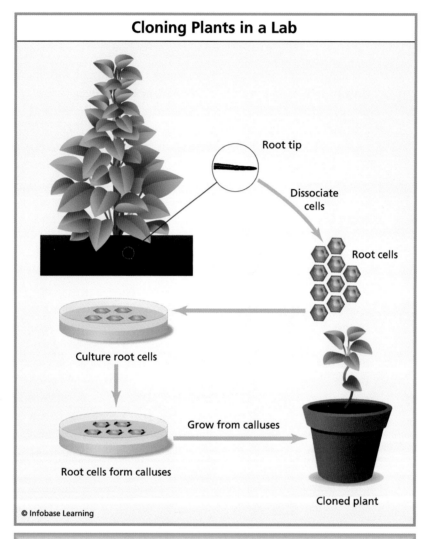

Figure 5.6 Cells from the root of an adult tree are used to clone new young trees.

garden in the village of Southwell, Nottinghamshire. One of the seeds contained the embryo that would grow into the original Bramley's Seedling apple tree. About 40 years later, local butcher and innkeeper Matthew Bramley bought the cottage and the garden with its apple tree. Bramley allowed local nurseryman Henry Merryweather to commercialize the apples as long as the fruit would be called a Bramley apple. Merryweather took grafts from the original tree to produce trees that grew Bramley apples. The grafting technique enabled Merryweather to grow Bramley apples by joining part of the Bramley apple tree to another apple tree. Over time, the Bramley apple became the world's most famous apple used for cooking.

Today, almost all Bramley apple trees are grafted cuttings of grafted cuttings obtained over many generations. In 1991, fungus and old age threatened the original Bramley apple tree. Scientists from The University of Nottingham in the United Kingdom cured the tree of the fungal infection and produced clones to preserve the original Bramley apple tree. The scientists removed shoot tips from the original tree, cut the tips into small pieces, and treated the tips to kill both the fungus and bacteria. Then, they grew plant tissue in the laboratory and planted clones in a glasshouse. By 2009, a dozen of the cloned Bramley apple trees thrived in a campus garden. "It is very interesting cultivating this unique collection of Bramley cloned from the original tree," said Desmond O'Grady, the university's grounds manager in a press release. "The trees in the orchard at The University of Nottingham provide a fine example of living history and a genetic bank for the future."

6

Cloning Animals

Cocoa Beach, Florida resident Kit Knotts owned a prized Lippizan stallion named Marc and wanted another horse exactly like him. "I called and emailed breeders to spread the word that I was looking," Knotts recalled in a press release from Texas A&M University at College Station. "Everything I could turn up was either too small, too young, too old, not quite sound, etc. I realized I didn't want just another horse to have another body in the barn, I wanted another Marc." The search for a new Marc led Knotts to Dr. Katrin Hinrichs, a professor in Texas A&M's Department of Veterinary Physiology & Pharmacology. After about two years of effort, Hinrichs and her colleagues produced a foal that is a clone of Marc. Knotts named the clone Mouse in honor of the cloning research with mice that provided the basis for cloning technology, and perhaps, in honor of Mouse's surrogate mother, a mare named Minnie.

In modern times, people have been turning to cloning technology to produce clones of their favorite animals. Pet owners fuel a small industry with their demands for cat and dog clones. Scientists are also using cloning technology to rescue threatened and endangered species. In 2001, for example, Pasqualino Loi of the University of Teramo, Italy and colleagues produced a clone of the nearly extinct European mouflon, one of the smallest wild sheep in the world. Scientists are trying to produce a clone from frozen skin of what may have been the last surviving bucardo, a type of Spanish ibex, which died in 2000. Will scientists soon create amusement parks inhabited by formerly extinct animals? David Wildt, a senior scientist at the Smithsonian National Zoological Park in Washington, D.C., advises that people should not get their hopes up. "The public should not leap to the conclusion that we are on the edge of cloning woolly mammoths or dinosaurs," he told *National Geographic*. "Even if such embryos could be constructed, there are no appropriate surrogate mothers for long-dead species."

However, while cloning pets and endangered species are interesting applications of cloning technology, the majority of practical cloning efforts center on the production of livestock clones to produce breeding stock with certain traits. Cloned livestock species include cattle, sheep, and swine. Farmers can use such clones as breeding animals to produce food-producing animals by conventional, sexual reproduction. The U.S. Food and Drug Administration (FDA) identifies five types of traits that breeders may want to see in clones used as breeding animals:

- **Increased resistance to disease**: A herd that can resist diseases would save a rancher veterinary costs and would avoid time lost in production of meat or milk due to the illness of the animal.
- **Increased suitability to climate**: The climate affects the ability of livestock to thrive. Ideally, breeders could choose clones able to flourish under local weather conditions. Suitability to climate could become a critical factor as global warming alters weather patterns.
- **Body form optimal for production function**: Meat-producing animals, for example, should be heavily-muscled animals that mature quickly to provide high-quality meat within a short time. Also, a large, well-attached udder is a useful trait for a dairy cow.
- **High fertility**: A high fertility rate ensures that farmers and ranchers can replace livestock slaughtered for meat.
- **Traits targeted to consumers**: Examples of currently preferred traits include lean and tender meat.

Cloning livestock represents a significant investment. In 2009, Barry Pollard, a neurosurgeon and ranch owner who had 22 clones in his cow herd, told *The Journal Record* that cloning a cow costs about $17,000. According to Blake Russell, vice-president

Clones on the Menu?

People invest money and time in livestock cloning to create clones that have desirable traits. Ranchers and farmers can use the clones as breeding animals that produce food-producing animals by conventional, sexual reproduction. During 2001, FDA officials asked researchers and livestock producers to prevent food from livestock clones or their offspring from entering the food supply until the agency confirmed the food was safe. In January 2008, the FDA announced that agency scientists concluded that meat and milk from clones of cows, pigs, and goats, as well as the offspring of any animal clones, are as safe to eat as food from conventionally bred animals. The FDA did not comment about the safety of food from clones of sheep and other animal species because the agency lacked sufficient information. Around the same time, the European Food Safety Authority (EFSA) announced that it had reached the same conclusions.

The decisions from the two agencies incited protests in the United States and in Europe. "To activists opposed to cloned food," *The Economist* reported, "the FDA and EFSA decisions mean only one thing: Frankenfoods are on their way. Since the creation of Dolly, a sheep cloned by researchers in Scotland in 1996, they have rallied many thousands to sign petitions and attend protest marches dressed as cloned cows and the like. And on the heels of this week's two big decisions, the anti-cloning crowd is kicking into high gear."

According to a 2007 editorial in *Nature Biotechnology*, food from clones is nothing new and here to stay. "Many common fruits (e.g., pears, apples, oranges and lemons) and several vegetables (e.g., potatoes and truffles) are clones," the editor wrote. "And most of us have probably ingested meat and dairy products from livestock cloned by natural reproduction (monozygotic siblings), mechanical embryo splitting or even nuclear transfer from an embryonic donor cell into an enucleated oocyte."

of ViaGen, an Austin, Texas-based cloning services company, livestock cloning costs are justified. "Livestock production is not an easy business, and one has to keep finding better ways to become more efficient," Russell told *The Journal Record*. "Cloning technology has become one of the most powerful tools in the industry to elevate the genetics of a herd and help nearly any livestock producer become more competitive."

ANIMAL CLONING TECHNOLOGY

The Techniques

One method for cloning livestock imitates the natural production of monozygotic twins. Monozygotic twins are created when one early embryo splits into two parts. Each half continues embryonic development, and twins are born. During the late 1970s, scientists introduced the cloning technique of embryo splitting. Cloning is performed by dividing an early embryo, usually in half, and transferring embryo segments to female animals that serve as surrogates for embryonic development. Embryo splitting has several limitations. The method typically produces only two clones; researchers rarely announce success after splitting an embryo into more segments. Another disadvantage of embryo splitting is that the technique produces clones that must mature before a farmer can determine if the clones have all of the desired traits.

Both disadvantages are overcome by a technique called somatic cell **nuclear transfer**, which has become the main cloning method. This technique earned international fame in 1997 when Ian Wilmut of Scotland's Roslin Institute announced the birth of a cloned sheep named Dolly. The sheep had been cloned with a nucleus from a mature sheep, marking the first time that scientists had cloned a vertebrate animal from an adult animal. Unlike embryo splitting, nuclear transfer can be used to produce many clones from the DNA of one animal. Furthermore, a scientist will know the clone's characteristics because the clone should be a copy of the mature animal that donates the DNA. In contrast, embryo splitting produces clones of an embryo, rather than clones of an animal with known traits.

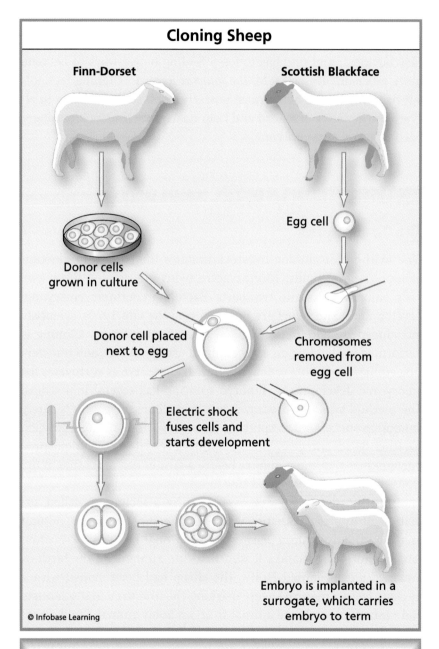

Cloning Sheep

Finn-Dorset

Scottish Blackface

Egg cell

Donor cells
grown in culture

Donor cell placed
next to egg

Chromosomes
removed from
egg cell

Electric shock
fuses cells and
starts development

© Infobase Learning

Embryo is implanted in a
surrogate, which carries
embryo to term

Figure 6.1   In this case of sheep cloning, the Finn-Dorset sheep
provides the nucleus, which is obtained from an udder cells. The
blackface provides the egg, which is subsequently enucleated. If the
cloning process is successful, the clone will look like a Finn-Dorset.

Wilmut and his colleagues produced Dolly by removing cells from the mammary gland of an adult Finn-Dorset sheep and transferring the cells to a culture dish. These cells served as nuclei donor cells. The cells were somatic cells, and therefore, the cells had diploid nuclei. The scientists then obtained oocytes from a Scottish Blackface sheep. The oocytes were arrested in the second stage of meiosis, which is the stage that oocytes become fertilized naturally. The scientists removed the nuclei of the oocytes, and then fused pairs of oocytes and nuclei donor cells by subjecting them to electric pulses. The "shock treatment" destabilized the cell membranes of donor cells and oocytes, enabling the membranes to fuse. The pulses also activated the fused cells to begin development into embryos. The scientists transferred each embryo into the uterus of a surrogate mother, another Scottish Blackface sheep. Dolly was born with

Figure 6.2 Dolly, the first genetically cloned mammal, is shown here as a lamb with its surrogate mother.

characteristics of a Finn-Dorset lamb, the strain of sheep that donated the nucleus. In time, Dolly gave birth to her own lamb, named Bonnie, by normal reproduction.

Limitations of Animal Cloning Methods

Although the idea of a nucleus swap performed by somatic cell nuclear transfer appears straightforward, the cloning success rate can be very low. Roslin Institute scientists experimented with 434 sheep oocytes before one gave rise to Dolly. In their 2010 *Journal of Reproduction and Development* article, Nguyen Van Thuan and colleagues from Konkuk University (South Korea) state that cloning efficiencies can vary from 0 to 20%. Even when the technique produces a clone, the animal may not be identical to the animal that donated the nucleus. Identical nucleotide sequences are insufficient to guarantee success in cloning.

Two cells with identical DNA can produce different proteins due to **epigenetic** effects. An epigenetic effect is a change in nuclear DNA that affects the activity of genes without changing nucleotide sequences in DNA. One type of epigenetic change is DNA methylation. In DNA methylation, an enzyme attaches a methyl group to a cytosine base in a DNA molecule. (A methyl group is a cluster of a carbon atom and three hydrogen atoms.) Attachment of methyl groups can interfere with the cell's machinery that synthesizes RNA from DNA, the process known as gene transcription. By interfering with gene transcription, methylation stops the production of the protein encoded by the gene. DNA methylation is reversible: Certain enzymes can remove methyl groups from cytosine bases.

Another type of epigenetic control involves proteins that bind with DNA. Each chromosome contains a single DNA molecule combined with histone proteins and nonhistone proteins. The combination of DNA and proteins is called chromatin. In chromatin, negatively charged DNA spools around positively charged histone proteins to create a structure like beads on a string. The beads-on-a-string chromatin is compacted further into a dense fiber-like structure called a solenoid. This compacting is necessary to squeeze billions of DNA base pairs into the cell nucleus.

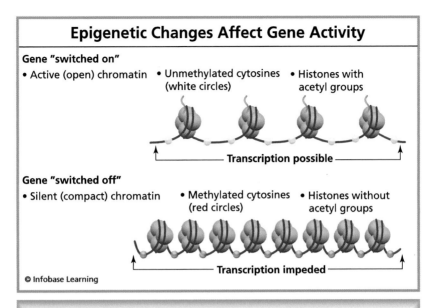

Epigenetic Changes Affect Gene Activity

Gene "switched on"
- Active (open) chromatin
- Unmethylated cytosines (white circles)
- Histones with acetyl groups

Transcription possible

Gene "switched off"
- Silent (compact) chromatin
- Methylated cytosines (red circles)
- Histones without acetyl groups

Transcription impeded

© Infobase Learning

Figure 6.3 This image shows changes in chromatin organization that influence gene expression. Genes are expressed, or switched on, when chromatin is open, or active. They are inactivated, or switched off, when the chromatin is condensed.

Chromatin structure affects the activities of genes. A dense, compact chromatin structure blocks enzymes from gaining access to a gene for transcription, making chromatin inactive. A relaxed, open structure allows transcription to take place, making the chromatin active. Chemical changes in histone proteins can affect whether chromatin is inactive or active. Scientists have found at least nine types of chemical changes in histones.

One example of a chemical change is the addition of acetyl groups to histones. An acetyl group is a cluster of one oxygen (O) atom, two carbon (C) atoms, and three hydrogen (H) atoms. Enzymes attach an acetyl group to an amino group on a histone. An amino group has a positive electrical charge and contains a nitrogen (N) atom and three hydrogen atoms. The addition of an acetyl group (CO-CH3) to an amino group (NH3+) abolishes the amino group's positive charge (NH-CO-CH3). Since the attachment of acetyl groups neutralizes the positive charge of histones, the attraction weakens between histones and negatively charged DNA. The weakened attraction causes chromatin structure to unravel, and allows transcription to take place. The reverse also happens. If an enzyme removes acetyl groups from histones, the proteins become more positively charged and bind more tightly to DNA. Removing acetyl groups can prevent transcription from a gene.

DNA methylation and changes in histones appear to be the main types of epigenetic changes in mammals. These two epigenetic modifications are often found together. Inactive genes often occur in methylated regions of DNA with dense chromatin and histones that lack acetyl groups. Active areas of chromatin can have unmethylated DNA and large amounts of histones with acetyl groups. Patterns of DNA methylation and histone changes can be passed on when cells divide.

Epigenetic alterations can also affect gene expression of an offspring's cells. This is a phenomenon named **genomic imprinting**: For a small number of genes, the parental source of a gene affects gene activity. Scientists chose the term "imprinting" to signal that something inactivates a gene without changing the nucleotide sequence of the gene. An imprinted gene is inactive in the sense that transcription from the gene is turned off. Two genes encoding the same protein can be active or inactive, depending upon whether it is inherited from the father or from the mother. That is, some genes have an imprint in the set of genes inherited from the mother, while other genes have an imprint in the set of genes inherited from the father. DNA methylation and other epigenetic alterations play a role in genomic imprinting.

A clone can also differ from its DNA donor due to a failure in **genetic reprogramming**, which may cause a clone to suffer health problems. In somatic cell nuclear transfer, the nucleus of a somatic cell is transferred into an egg cell, which then progresses through embryonic development. The technique's success depends upon a reprogramming of gene expression activities in the nucleus of a mature, somatic cell so that gene activities are appropriate to provide the molecules required for growth of a young embryo. During a "reboot," a nucleus turns off many genes that are active in the somatic cell and turns on genes that support developmental processes.

CASE STUDY: CLONING FAVORITE PETS TO RECREATE UNIQUENESS

In 1997, Arizona entrepreneur John Sperling investigated the possibility of cloning Missy, his family's mixed-breed dog. Sperling's Missyplicity Project became a $3.7 million effort, which helped to fund a cloning research program at Texas A&M University. Cloning dogs proved to be difficult, so researchers at Texas A&M's College of Veterinary Medicine used nuclear transfer to attempt to clone a cat as part of the Missyplicity Project. After 188 failures, they announced in December 2001 that they had produced the first cloned companion animal, a kitten named CC (for "carbon copy"). Although CC is a clone of Rainbow and both are female calico cats, the animals differ in appearance due to an effect called **X chromosome inactivation**.

Most female mammals have two X chromosomes in the nucleus of each somatic cell, whereas most males have one X chromosome and one Y chromosome. If a female embryo's cells express genes from both X chromosomes, the embryo can suffer abnormalities. This problem caused by too much gene expression is avoided by the inactivation of one X chromosome in each cell during early embryonic development. Inactivation of an X chromosome in a particular cell—either the X chromosome inherited from the mother or the X chromosome inherited from the father—appears to be random. As a cell divides by mitosis, the same X chromosome will be inactivated in daughter cells. Consequently, female mammals are said to possess a mosaic of somatic cells due to the random inactivation of X chromosomes.

The blend of coat colors of a calico cat illustrates the mosaic effect. The X chromosome of a calico cat has a gene that causes the production of either yellow fur or black fur. The mosaic effect results in a coat color pattern due to patches of skin cells that produce yellow or black fur depending upon which X chromosome is active. Random inactivation of X chromosomes ensures that a cloned female calico cat such as CC will not be identical to the animal that donated a nucleus.

The Missyplicity Project expanded into a company called Genetic Savings and Clone, which was located in Sausalito, California.

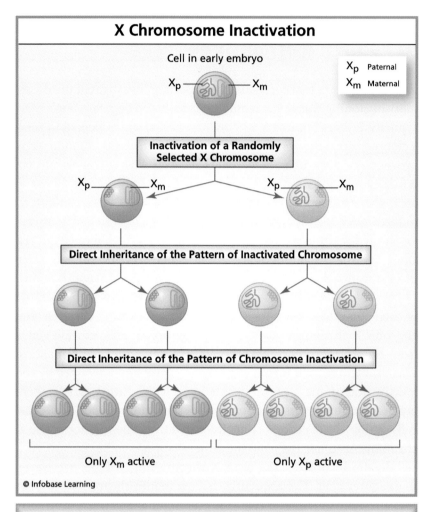

Figure 6.4 This illustration shows how daughter cells inherit an inactive X chromosome.

The company pursued the cloning of pets and especially Missy. During 2005, scientist Woo-Suk Hwang and his colleagues at Seoul National University's College of Veterinary Medicine, in South Korea, announced that they had used nuclear transfer to produce the first cloned dog, a male Afghan hound puppy clone named Snuppy. Although Missy died in 2002, BioArts International, of Mill Valley, California, and the Sooam Biotech Research Foundation, of Seoul,

South Korea, produced four Missy clones during 2007 and 2008: Mira, MissyToo, Mani, and Kahless.

Some people have paid at least $50,000 per cloned cat and more than $150,000 for a cloned dog. Writing for msnbc.com, Ursula Masterson reported that pet cloning company executives offer several warnings to potential clients about their expensive pet clones. "For instance," Masterson wrote, "they remind them that the clone will not be the same pet, but rather a completely new animal with identical genes. It will definitely not have the same 'memories,' and may not even have exactly the same temperament." Masterson said that most "pet owners eager to clone don't seem concerned about such details, however. As long as the general look, build, and above all temperament are similar, they say, they'll feel satisfied that some part of their beloved pet is 'living on.'"

Arlene Judith Klotzko, a writer at the Science Museum, in London, offered a more skeptical view of pet cloning in *The Cloning Sourcebook* (2001). "A wonderful paradox lies behind the Missyplicity Project," she wrote. "Its rich benefactor has asked that scientists employ a technique that many see as a threat to uniqueness in a futile quest to perpetuate a unique life by reconstructing a new dog." Klotzko advises that "Those who seek reincarnation must look to metaphysics—not genetics."

CLONING HUMANS?

There is one type of clone that occurs naturally in humans: the identical twin. Monozygotic twins, or identical twins, occur when the cells of a single embryo separate and form two embryos. In contrast, dizygotic twins, or fraternal twins, result from the fertilization of two egg cells. Like artificially produced clones, identical twins are not necessarily identical. Random events during development can affect identical twins, such as X chromosome inactivation. Differences in an embryo's immediate environment also affect the development of twins. For example, identical twins develop in unique microenvironments within the uterus, which influence the formation of ridge patterns in fingertip skin. As a result, identical twins do not have the same fingerprints. Scientists have also found that identical

Cloning Around

For more than 30 years, people have claimed success in the creation of a human clone. For the same amount of time, scientists have denounced such claims as hoaxes.

In 1978, readers of the New York Post were greeted with the headline "Baby Born without a Mother: He's First Human Clone." The article reported information from a forthcoming book, In His Image: The Cloning of Man. Science reporter David Rorvik, the book's author, told a story about his encounter with a California millionaire who hired Rorvik to establish a laboratory on a Pacific Island. A science team labored for years before a surrogate mother gave birth to healthy boy, an infant cloned from one of the millionaire's cells. Rorvik supported his amazing story with a description of research by Dr. J. Derek Bromhall, who had been a biologist at Oxford University and had invented a method for performing nuclear transfer in mammalian cells. Legislators responded to the news by demanding a ban on human cloning. After studying the details of the human cloning claim, however, scientists declared a hoax. Three years after publication, a judge agreed that the book was a fictional account of human cloning that included Bromhall's genuine research; the book's publisher publicly apologized to Bromhall.

twins have differences in their genomes due to the loss of segments of DNA and the gain of extra copies of DNA segments.

Artificially produced human clones have populated science fiction stories for many decades. However, there are two technologies that, when combined, may enable real human **reproductive cloning**: in vitro fertilization procedures and somatic cell nuclear transfer. Theoretically, human cloning might be performed by extracting the nucleus from a human egg cell and replacing it with a nucleus removed from a somatic cell of the person to be cloned. Following nuclear transfer, the artificially produced zygote would be allowed to develop into an early stage embryo while bathed in nutrient

During December 2002, representatives of the Raelians, a religious sect, announced that they had produced a human clone, a baby named Eve, in collaboration with a company called Clonaid. The news led to a demand for proof that Eve was a real clone. Dr. Michael A. Guillen, a former ABC News science editor, was brought in to coordinate testing with a team of scientists who would examine the DNA of the allegedly cloned baby. Guillen said that Clonaid had offered him complete freedom in the validation process. However, a month later, he was less than optimistic—he had not been given access to the supposed clone. "[I]t's still entirely possible," Guillen told *The New York Times*, "Clonaid's announcement is part of an elaborate hoax intended to bring publicity to the Raelian movement."

Bioengineering experts Kyle Kurpinski and Terry Johnson have mulled over the day when human cloning becomes not only feasible, but also popular. According to their book, *How to Defeat Your Own Clone* (2010), conflicts will arise between original humans and their clones. "Think you can outsmart yourself?" they ask. "Think you can beat yourself in a fight? Think it can't happen to you? Think again, bub. The first rule of cloning is: Don't ever let your clone read this book."

medium in a culture dish. The human embryo would be implanted in a surrogate mother to create a clone of the person who donated the nucleus.

Why clone a human? In 2002, The National Academies, in the United States, published a report on human reproductive cloning, in which the group identified three reasons why people might decide to produce a child by reproductive cloning:

- A couple may want to have a child that is genetically identical with one of them, or identical to someone else.
- Parents who have lost a child may want to produce a child who is genetically identical to that lost child.

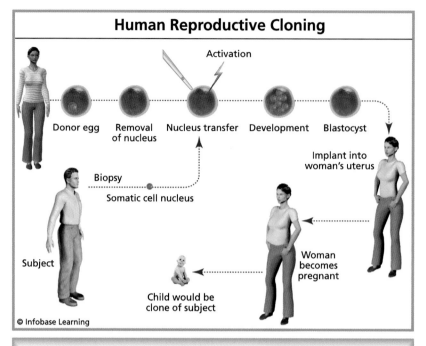

Figure 6.5 Human reproductive cloning is illegal in some countries.

 * Individuals who need a tissue transplant to treat their own disease or a disease of their child may decide to create a clone who has genetically identical tissue.

These motivations for human cloning have stirred protests on ethical grounds.

TO CLONE OR NOT TO CLONE?

Experiments with animal cloning have highlighted that identical genomes alone are not enough to ensure that two animals will be identical. Other factors that affect gene expression come into play, such as epigenetic control of gene expression, genomic imprinting, genetic reprogramming, and X chromosome inactivation. Cloning efforts have been plagued by low success rates and the production of cloned animals with increased susceptibility to infections, high rates of tumor growth, anemia, obesity, heart disorders, respiratory failure, and other health problems. North Carolina State University researchers, for example, discovered a link between three imprinted genes and long-term harmful health effects in cloned pigs. Animal cloning experiments provoke concerns about animal welfare.

Many people forcefully oppose human reproductive cloning. "It is dangerous, profoundly wrong, and has no place in our society, or any society," asserted President Barack Obama. In 2002, the President's Council on Bioethics concluded that reproductive cloning is unsafe and morally unacceptable. The council voiced concern that cloning would violate the principles of human research ethics because the technology posed serious risks of birth defects and long-term health problems; that cloned children could experience problems of identity, because each child would be virtually identical—genetically, at least—to another person; and that, if human cloning became an accepted practice, then society may view cloned children as the products of manufacture, which would reduce human dignity.

In 1997, science writer Arlene Klotzko interviewed Dr. Grahame Bulfield, the director and chief executive of the Roslin Institute and honorary professor of genetics at the University of Edinburgh. In this interview for her article in *The Cloning Sourcebook*, Klotzko asked the director of the institute that produced Dolly about the moral acceptability of cloning of human beings. "The general view that we have taken on the cloning of human beings is a fivefold stance," Bulfield replied. "First, we don't know whether we can do it on humans. Second, we have no intention of doing it on humans. Third, we don't believe that there is any justified clinical reason for doing it on humans. Fourth, we have no intention of licensing our technology for anybody to do it on humans. Fifth, it is illegal, at least in Britain."

In 2002, The National Academies recommended that the U.S. government should also place a ban on the practice of human reproductive cloning, a technology that the group called dangerous and likely to fail. The National Academies did not urge a permanent ban, but rather recommended a periodic review of a law that would prohibit human cloning. "The ban should be reconsidered," the group suggested, "only if at least two conditions are met: (1) a new scientific and medical review indicates that the procedures are likely to be safe and effective and (2) a broad national dialogue on the societal, religious, and ethical issues suggests that a reconsideration of the ban is warranted."

Engineering Reproduction

S cientists have combined techniques for controlling reproductive processes of plants and animals with methods for altering a cell's genome. Known as the science of genetic engineering, these techniques enable researchers to produce modified plants and animals with new traits. Genetic engineering relies upon **recombinant DNA** technology. Recombinant DNA is DNA that has been altered in the laboratory by the addition or deletion of nucleotide sequences.

Scientists who work in this field, the "genetic engineers," possess at least four important tools in their toolkits: transgenes, vectors, restriction enzymes, and ligases. Often, the goal of genetic engineering is to remove a gene from the chromosome of one organism and transfer this foreign gene into another organism. The transferred gene is called a **transgene**, while an organism that receives a transgene may be called a **transgenic** organism or a genetically engineered organism. A transgene is transferred to a cell using a DNA molecule called a **vector**. One type of vector is a plasmid, which is a small, circular DNA molecule that replicates itself in bacterial cells.

Scientists use restriction enzymes and ligases to insert a transgene into a vector. A restriction enzyme is an enzyme that cuts DNA at a specific (restricted) place. A restriction enzyme glides along the backbone of a DNA molecule until it comes across a certain

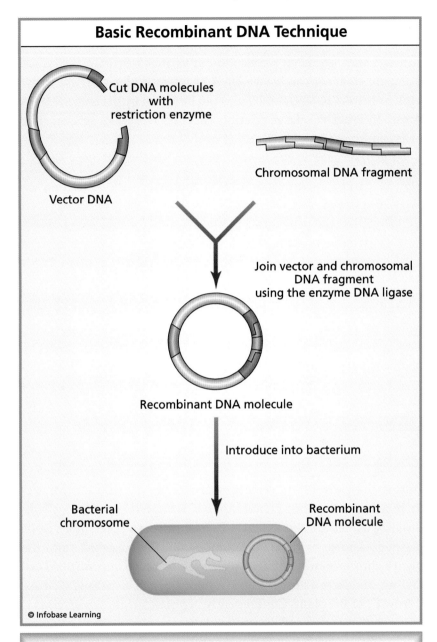

Basic Recombinant DNA Technique

Cut DNA molecules
with
restriction enzyme

Chromosomal DNA fragment

Vector DNA

Join vector and chromosomal
DNA fragment
using the enzyme DNA ligase

Recombinant DNA molecule

Introduce into bacterium

Bacterial
chromosome

Recombinant
DNA molecule

© Infobase Learning

Figure 7.1   In a basic recombinant DNA technique, DNA sequences
that would not normally occur together are combined.

target nucleotide sequence that is called its cleavage site. There, the
enzyme binds to the DNA molecule. Once the enzyme has the DNA
backbone in its firm grasp, the enzyme twists into a different shape.

As the enzyme contorts, it distorts the DNA molecule and breaks the DNA backbone. Different restriction enzymes bind to different cleavage sites. By using a collection of various restriction enzymes, a genetic engineer can cleave DNA at selected places. These cleavages, or breaks, in DNA molecules can be sealed by the enzyme DNA ligase. In other words, restriction enzymes work like scissors, and ligase enzymes work like glue.

The basic genetic engineering process has three steps:

1. Cleave a gene from a DNA molecule with restriction enzymes.
2. Splice the gene into a plasmid or other vector using restriction enzymes and DNA ligase.
3. Insert the vector into a host cell to produce a transgenic cell.

Initially, scientists used this process to produce genetically engineered bacteria that synthesized new proteins and RNA molecules. Today, researchers apply the technology to alter many types of plants, but especially those that are grown for food.

GENETIC ENGINEERING OF PLANTS

Methods for Engineering Plants

During the early 1980s, scientists devised a way to use a parasite to produce transgenic plants. *Agrobacterium tumefaciens*, a soil-dwelling bacteria, infects plant cells by inserting a portion of a DNA plasmid—known as the Ti or "tumor inducing" plasmid—into the plant's chromosomes. Infected plant cells undergo uncontrolled cell division and form a growth called a tumor or gall, usually at the base ("crown") of the plant. Consequently, *Agrobacterium tumefaciens* is said to inflict crown gall disease in plants.

In one approach to creating transgenic plants, scientists disarm the Ti plasmid by removing nucleotide sequences that cause crown gall disease. A researcher then constructs a small plasmid vector with transgenes and inserts the small vector into a disarmed Ti plasmid. As an example, a researcher could prepare a small plasmid vector using the restriction enzyme *Bam*HI, the first restriction enzyme originally isolated from the bacterium **Bacillus amyloliquefaciens H**. This enzyme seeks out the nucleotide sequence GGATCC. *Bam*HI breaks a DNA molecule after the first guanine (G) nucleotide in the cleavage site. In a double-stranded DNA molecule, the cleavage site would appear as follows:

.... GGATCC ....

.... CCTAGG ....

In this example, *Bam*HI cuts open a circular plasmid. Cleavage of the DNA leaves two short stubs of single-stranded DNA, called "sticky ends." Sticky ends can form base pairs with themselves or with matching pieces of DNA.

.... G GATCC ....

.... CCTAG G ....

*Bam*HI is used to remove a transgene from a chromosome, creating two sticky ends.

GATCC .... G

G .... CCTAG

After mixing the cleaved plasmid and transgene, the two types of DNA fit together like pieces of a puzzle by forming base pairs at the sticky ends.

.... GGATCC .... GGATCC ....

.... CCTAGG .... CCTAGG ....

Finally, DNA ligase seals the breaks in the DNA molecules.

A researcher adds vector DNA that contains one or more transgenes to a culture of *Agrobacterium*, which have disarmed Ti plasmids. Vector DNA enters bacterial cells and inserts into Ti plasmids. Small pieces of plant tissue are placed in culture dishes and infected with the *Agrobacterium*. In some plant cells, Ti plasmid DNA, with its transgenes, inserts into plant chromosomes. So far, the method can be summarized as follows:

Construct small plasmid vector with transgenes

↓

Add small vector to *Agrobacterium* so that the vector
inserts into a disarmed Ti plasmid

↓

Infect cultured plant cells with the *Agrobacterium*

At this point, a researcher has a mixture of plant cells: Some cells contain transgenes and some do not. It is now time to kill those cells that lack transgenes with an antibiotic, such as kanamycin, which carries out this task by blocking protein synthesis. Researchers often include a kanamycin resistance gene as one of the transgenes. The kanamycin resistance gene encodes an enzyme that inactivates kanamycin. Plant cells that have functional transgenes in their chromosomes synthesize the enzyme that inactivates kanamycin so that the cells survive drug treatment. The drug-resistant cells divide and grow into a cluster of non-specialized cells called a callus. By adjusting nutrients and hormones, a researcher can stimulate a callus to form shoots and roots, and to develop into plantlets. The small plants are transferred to soil and develop into transgenic plants. Note that all cells of a transgenic plant should contain transgenes within the chromosomes. As a result, a transgenic plant should produce gametes that also contain the transgenes.

Using a modified Ti plasmid to create a transgenic plant is a lengthy process. Another popular technique for producing a transgenic plant is microprojectile bombardment, or *biolistics*, a method in which DNA is shot into a plant cell. The method is performed with DNA-coated gold particles that have diameters of about 0.000032 inches (0.8 microns). The particles are loaded into a gene gun, and high-pressure helium gas propels the DNA-coated pellets into plant cells at speeds up to 2,000 feet per second (600 meters per second). After DNA-coated particles burst through a plant cell wall, DNA molecules are released from the particles and become inserted within plant cell chromosomes.

Various Types of Transgenic Plants

In 1996, farmers planted the first significant large-scale transgenic crop. During 2010, according to the International Service for the

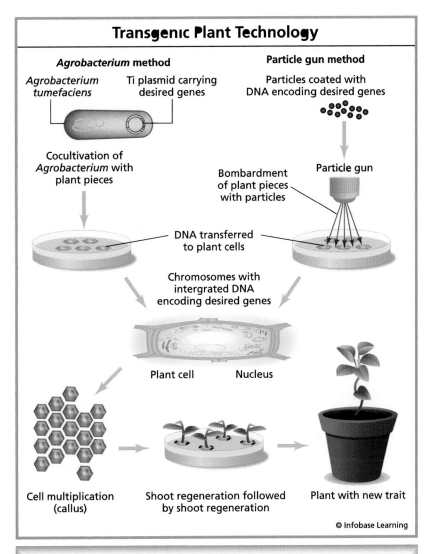

Transgenic Plant Technology

Agrobacterium method

Particle gun method

Agrobacterium tumefaciens

Ti plasmid carrying desired genes

Particles coated with DNA encoding desired genes

Cocultivation of *Agrobacterium* with plant pieces

Bombardment of plant pieces with particles

Particle gun

DNA transferred to plant cells

Chromosomes with intergrated DNA encoding desired genes

Plant cell   Nucleus

Cell multiplication (callus)

Shoot regeneration followed by shoot regeneration

Plant with new trait

© Infobase Learning

Figure 7.2 A transgenic plant contains genes that have been artificially inserted in order to produce a new plant with specific traits.

Acquisition of Agri-biotech Applications, 15.4 million farmers in 29 countries planted 365 million acres (148 million hectares) of transgenic crops. Farmers in the United States grew a little over 45% of this acreage. The U.S. Department of Agriculture reported that the majority of corn (86%), cotton (93%), and soybeans (93%) planted by U.S. farmers in 2010 had been genetically altered.

Many of the first transgenic crops produce proteins that kill insect pests. This eliminates the need for farmers to spray crops with traditional chemical insecticides, which are not only costly for farmers but also harmful to the environment. For example, certain genetically engineered crops synthesize toxic proteins produced by the soil-dwelling bacterium, *Bacillus thuringiensis*. These toxic proteins typically kill a limited number of insect species and do not directly affect other animals. During 2010, a group of scientists led by entomologist William Hutchison of the University of Minnesota, in St. Paul, published their study on the benefits of cultivating transgenic corn that synthesizes a toxic protein that kills an insect called the European corn borer. U.S. farmers began to grow the transgenic corn in 1996. Due to a decreased need for insecticides by using this corn, farmers in the five surveyed states (Iowa, Minnesota, Illinois, Wisconsin, and Nebraska) saved almost $6.9 billion. Since the transgenic corn has decreased populations of the European corn borer, farmers who grow conventional, non-transgenic corn have also reaped the benefits provided by crops of insecticide-producing transgenic corn.

Certain transgenic traits enable plants to survive under harsh conditions. Drought, for example, is a reoccurring problem for African farmers, who face the possibility that a lack of water will cause their crops to wither and die. In Africa, the most widely-grown staple crop is corn, which is sensitive to dry conditions. The Water Efficient Maize for Africa project developed transgenic, drought-tolerant corn. During November and December of 2010, farmers planted drought-tolerant transgenic corn in test fields located in Uganda and Kenya.

Other transgenic plants have been designed to increase their flavor or nutritional content. For instance, golden rice is transgenic rice that contains beta-carotene in the grain. Although the human body cannot make its own vitamin A, human cells can convert beta-carotene to vitamin A. (People who live on a diet with little beta-carotene risk vitamin A shortage, which can cause such health problems as blindness, severe infections, and life-threatening diseases.) Golden rice contains two transgenes: One gene is obtained from a soil bacterium and the other is obtained from daffodil or maize. The transgenes encode enzymes that work together to produce beta-carotene. With its yellow-orange color, golden rice stands out from ordinary white rice.

Other types of transgenic crops have been engineered to synthesize proteins and chemicals for medicine and industry. These genetic engineering efforts are often called molecular farming, or *biopharming*, and can provide a means to produce therapeutic proteins and chemicals at lower cost and in greater amounts than traditional methods.

The production of transgenic crops has incited longstanding protests. People who object to genetically engineered crops often argue that scientists who apply genetic modification tread in realms best left to the Creator. In 1998, Prince Charles, the British Prince of Wales, published his views on this issue in the London newspaper *The Daily Telegraph*. "The fundamental difference between traditional and genetically modified plant breeding is that, in the latter, genetic material from one species of plant, bacteria, virus, animal or fish is literally inserted into another species, with which they could never naturally breed," he wrote. "I happen to believe that this kind of genetic modification takes mankind into realms that belong to God, and to God alone."

Those who oppose transgenic crops also highlight possible risks to human health and the environment. One argument against transgenic crops is that altering genes might accidentally enable a plant to produce a molecule toxic to humans. Another argument is that cultivating transgenic plants that make insecticidal proteins could harm the environment by killing insects that do not feed on crops. The death of these non-target insects would affect birds, fish, and other animals that eat the insects.

Yet another basis for protests against transgenic crops is that the plants may spread outside of their fields. In 2010, scientists presented the first evidence that transgenic canola plants established populations outside of their original fields. They also found two cases in which canola plants contained multiple transgenes, which suggests that different types of genetically engineered plants can breed in the wild to produce new types of transgenic plants. The study supports protestors who have claimed that farmers cannot contain transgenic crops and their transgenes.

Certain transgenes, such as genes that provide resistance to insects or disease-causing viruses, increase the fitness of transgenic plants. If these advantageous transgenes spread into populations of conventional plants, then new types of transgenic plants could

Plant Blanches to Signal Danger

Biologists at Colorado State University in Fort Collins have engineered plants to create an early warning system for the presence of explosives. "The idea to make detector plants comes directly from nature," biologist June Medford explained in a press release. "Plants can't run or hide from threats, so they've developed sophisticated systems to detect and respond to their environment. We've 'taught' plants how to detect things we're interested in and respond in a way anyone can see, to tell us there is something nasty around."

Medford and her team "rewired" a plant's natural signaling process so that the leaves turn from green to white when the plant detects the presence of TNT, the most commonly used explosive. Plants have proteins called receptors that detect certain chemicals in the environment when the chemicals bind with the receptors. With the help of a computer program, the Colorado State University team redesigned plant receptors to bind with TNT. After engineering a gene encoding the redesigned receptor, they produced a transgenic plant that had the new receptors in its cell walls. The binding of TNT with the receptors stimulates a chain of events leading to a loss of the green pigment chlorophyll from the leaves. Consequently, the leaves turn white, signaling the presence of TNT.

In their experiments, the researchers found that the plants reacted to TNT levels one one-hundredth of an amount that a bomb-sniffing dog could detect. However, the plant detection system needs tweaking. The color change takes hours, whereas a practical warning system should respond within minutes. Engineering a quick response is possible, Medford says, but the project may require three to seven years of further experiments. One day, explosive-detecting plants may be used to protect soldiers from improvised explosive devices (IEDs), and provide another type of security in airports. Transgenic plants may also be designed to detect environmental pollutants.

become dominant in the environment, killing off conventional plants. The net result would be a loss of biological diversity, or *biodiversity*. (Biodiversity is a concept that refers to the variety and abundance of living things on Earth.)

GENETIC ENGINEERING OF ANIMALS

In a December 1982 article in the journal *Nature*, scientists Richard Palmiter, from the University of Washington at Seattle, Ralph Brinster from the University of Pennsylvania, Philadelphia and their colleagues reported the production of the first transgenic mouse. The researchers injected a modified rat growth hormone gene into fertilized mouse eggs and then transferred the eggs into a mouse that acted as a surrogate mother. Although all of the pups were of normal size at birth, some of them rapidly grew to nearly twice the size of their littermates under the influence of the growth hormone transgene. The Palmiter-Brinster team used the technique of DNA microinjection to engineer these transgenic mice. The technique is performed by allowing a sperm cell to fuse with an egg cell in a laboratory culture dish. Before the two nuclei fuse, a scientist injects a piece of DNA into one of the nuclei. The DNA fragment, which includes one or more transgenes, inserts into the chromosomes. The nuclei fuse and the cell continues to develop as an embryo.

Using a variety of techniques, scientists have engineered many types of transgenic mice, as well as transgenic insects, fish, goats, sheep, chickens, cows, rabbits, and pigs. One popular method for producing transgenic animals requires a vector made from a virus. A normal virus carries the instructions in its genetic material to reproduce itself, but lacks the means to do so. Instead, a virus must infect a cell and take over the cell's protein and nucleic acid synthesis machinery to make copies of itself. To construct a vector, scientists alter a virus's genetic material by removing genes for virus reproduction. Then, they add one or more transgenes. A virus vector can efficiently deliver transgenes to the chromosomes of young animal embryos. Other genetic engineering methods include the insertion of transgenes into sperm cells before fertilization, and the genetic modification of somatic cell nuclei before somatic cell nuclear transfer.

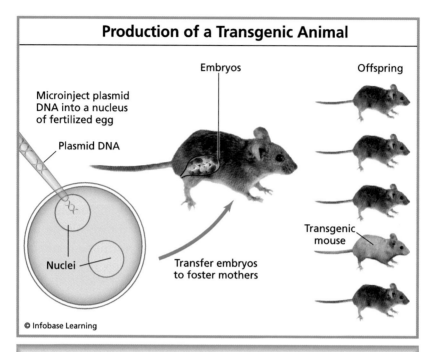

Production of a Transgenic Animal

Microinject plasmid
DNA into a nucleus
of fertilized egg

Plasmid DNA

Nuclei

Embryos

Transfer embryos
to foster mothers

Offspring

Transgenic
mouse

© Infobase Learning

Figure 7.3 To produce a transgenic animal, DNA is microinjected into a nucleus of a fertilized egg. The microinjected eggs are then transferred to foster mothers and allowed to develop. Some of the offspring are transgenic, in that they have incorporated the injected DNA into their genome.

Researchers produce transgenic animals for a variety of purposes. Some transgenic animals are designed for research into basic questions of biology, and others provide animal models for study of the causes of human diseases and to test possible treatments. For example, transgenic pigs have been engineered so that scientists can study diseases, such as cystic fibrosis, and to test methods for treating damage to arteries caused by high cholesterol blood levels.

Transgenic livestock have a variety of new traits, such as transgenic cows that synthesize protein-enriched milk, and transgenic pigs that provide more healthful types of meat. Researchers at the University of Guelph, in Ontario, Canada, developed a pig that synthesizes a bacterial enzyme, which allows the animals to absorb more phosphorus from feed. The transgenic pigs excrete less phosphorus and so decrease the amount of pollution generated by conventional pigs.

Other research efforts aim to produce transgenic livestock that resist diseases or stop the spread of disease from animals to humans. For example, scientists have been designing livestock that resist mad cow disease. Researchers have also targeted the avian flu, which spreads among chickens and can infect humans. The 1997 avian flu threat started in Hong Kong with a bird flu virus that caused an outbreak of serious disease in poultry. Eighteen people also became infected from chickens and six of them died. Years later, avian flu viruses appeared in a number of Asian countries, Europe, and Africa. In 2011, researchers at the Universities of Cambridge and Edinburgh announced that they had produced transgenic chickens that cannot transmit avian flu virus to other chickens. By stopping virus transmission, this accomplishment can prevent flu outbreak from spreading within a flock and reduce the risk of a further transfer of viruses to humans.

Some transgenic animals synthesize pharmaceuticals. For example, transgenic pigs, goats, sheep, and cattle have been engineered to secrete protein drugs into their milk. The therapeutic proteins can be isolated from the milk, purified, and used as medicines for humans. In 2009, the U.S. Food and Drug Administration approved the first drug produced by transgenic livestock that have a human gene. Genetically engineered goats synthesize a human protein called antithrombin, which can prevent life-threatening blood clots. Technicians purify the therapeutic protein from the transgenic goats' milk.

Researchers have applied genetic engineering technology to improve xenotransplantation, which is a type of therapy in which tissue from a nonhuman is transplanted into a human. The goal of xenotransplantation is to alleviate the severe shortage of human organs available for transplant. A difficulty with xenotransplants is that the human immune system attacks cells that are foreign to the body, including cells from a nonhuman animal. Genetic engineering can provide a means to modify nonhuman tissue so that it does not incite an immune system attack after transplant. For instance, scientists have engineered transgenic pigs with human proteins on their cells, which should prevent an immune attack after pig tissue is transplanted into humans.

Another application of genetic engineering is to control insect pests and disease-causing organisms. Researchers are engineering insects in a variety of ways, such as altering cotton plant-eating pink bollworms to carry a gene that would prevent offspring from developing, and modification of bacteria in the kissing bug's gut to kill the parasite that causes Chagas' disease.

Genetic engineers also target disease-spreading mosquitoes. *Aedes aegypti* mosquitoes transmit dengue virus infection, which is a leading cause of illness and death in the tropics and subtropics. Scientists at Oxitec Ltd., a biotechnology company based in Oxford, England, developed transgenic *Aedes aegypti* mosquitoes to stop the spread of dengue virus. They engineered male mosquitoes to transfer a gene that kills the insect at the larval stage of its lifecycle and curbs populations of mosquito carriers of the virus. During 2010, the company performed a field trial in the Cayman Islands, releasing about 3 million transgenic male mosquitoes. (Male mosquitoes were used because they do not draw blood and infect humans.) Oxitec reported that the local population of *Aedes aegypti* mosquito decreased by 80%.

The genetic engineering of animals has fueled protests for decades. Many claim that it is unethical to modify animals with recombinant DNA technology. Although humans have altered animals by selective breeding for thousands of years, genetic engineering differs from traditional breeding methods in several significant ways. Unlike traditional methods that require generations to achieve the desired results, the new technology can create striking alterations in a single generation. Another difference between the two approaches is that in traditional breeding, the selected trait may be accompanied by a number of genes that support the desired trait. With genetic engineering, a desired trait may require a single transgene. The introduction of this single, new gene may disrupt the normal balance of traits within the transgenic animal. For example, scientists have developed transgenic salmon that have an extra growth hormone gene and grow twice as fast as conventional (non-transgenic) salmon. However, rapidly-growing transgenic salmon sometimes develop severe deformities, such as disfigurements of the skull. This type of unintended effect in the creation of transgenic animals has led to objections to genetic engineering based on animal welfare concerns.

The engineering of farm animals has also stirred anxiety about food safety. A transgenic animal may synthesize new proteins, which may be included in food produced from the animals. Will the new proteins cause an allergic reaction in people who consume the food? The U.S. Food and Drug Administration monitors food safety, including the possibility that food from transgenic animals may spark an allergic reaction.

Transgenic animals also present environmental issues. If transgenic animals escape into the wild, they could spread their transgenes by mating with non-transgenic animals of the same species. By the time that an unintended spread of transgenes is detected, it may be too late to remedy the situation. Transgenic animals might replace their non-transgenic counterparts.

GENETIC ENGINEERING OF HUMANS

A person's genome affects the risk of developing a disease. A genetic disease results from DNA mutations that create abnormal nucleotide sequences in a person's genome. Genetic mutations can lead to disease in two general ways. Sometimes, a mutation in a gene directly causes illness by affecting a protein vital for health. Other genetic diseases arise from a combination of factors: A DNA mutation that places a person at risk for a disease may be followed by exposure to something in the environment that promotes the development of a disorder. Disease-causing environmental factors include infection by certain viruses, exposure to certain toxic chemicals, and overexposure to the sun's ultraviolet light.

One general type of genetic disease is the single-gene disorder, which is caused by a mutation in one gene. Scientists have identified more than 10,000 human single-gene diseases, such as sickle cell anemia, galactosemia, and cystic fibrosis. In a single-gene disease, the protein encoded by the mutated gene may be synthesized in an altered form, or the protein may not be synthesized at all.

For more than 20 years, scientists and physicians have been testing gene therapies to treat single-gene diseases. To perform gene therapy, a scientist must develop a delivery system to carry a transgene to the patient's cells. Genetically engineered viruses have proved to be a popular type of delivery system. A scientist typically modifies the genetic material of a virus in at least two ways: (1) delete nucleotide sequences that contain instructions for making copies

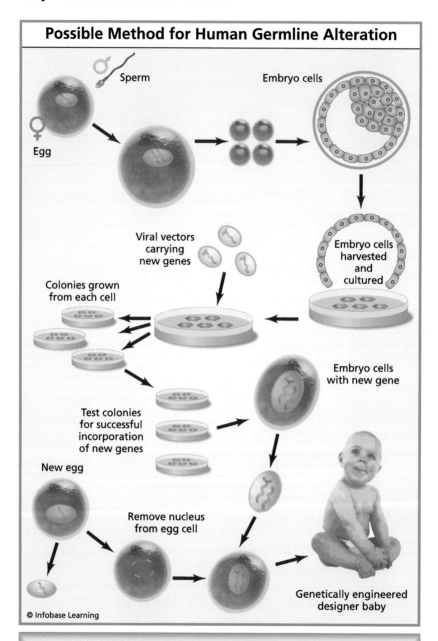

Possible Method for Human Germline Alteration

Sperm

Embryo cells

Egg

Viral vectors carrying new genes

Embryo cells harvested and cultured

Colonies grown from each cell

Embryo cells with new gene

Test colonies for successful incorporation of new genes

New egg

Remove nucleus from egg cell

Genetically engineered designer baby

© Infobase Learning

Figure 7.4 This proposed method for germline genetic modification combines genetic engineering and cloning techniques.

of the virus, and (2) add nucleotide sequences that encode the transgene. The genetically engineered virus delivers the transgene to the cells. Once inside the cells, the virus's nucleic acid molecule inserts into the cell's chromosomes, and the transgene enables cells to produce the therapeutic protein.

This approach to gene therapy is sometimes called somatic gene therapy, because the technique introduces a transgene into somatic cells, such as white blood cells. Some people have raised a concern that somatic gene therapy could accidentally result in the transfer of transgenes into egg cells or sperm cells. If this occurred, then the transgene would be passed on to future generations. The ultimate objective of a technique called germline genetic modification is the deliberate introduction of a transgene into egg or sperm cells. The goal of this approach would be to cure a genetic disease in a family, and even to eliminate a genetic disease from the human population.

So far, germline genetic modification of humans has remained a theory. Nevertheless, the idea has incited controversy. One ethical concern about germline genetic modification centers on consent. In the United States and many other countries, researchers must inform a potential subject about the risks posed by an experimental treatment, and then the researchers must obtain voluntary consent from the potential subject who wants to participate in the study. Germline genetic modification presents unknowable risks. A transgene may insert into chromosomes, resulting in disease or a lethal outcome. In addition, the technique affects future generations, who clearly cannot give their consent.

Religious commentators have expressed approval of somatic cell gene therapy because of its goal of treating disease in an individual. However, this has not been the case for germline genetic modification, which would, theoretically, treat a disease by altering the genomes of people as yet unborn. Advocates of germline genetic modification have been accused of "playing God." A related concern about germline genetic modification is that the technique could be used to manufacture humans to desired specifications, which would diminish human dignity. For example, the technology might be used to "upgrade" intelligence, athletic performance, and other traits.

Feelings about germline genetic modification of humans run so strongly that Australia, Canada, Germany, and other countries have declared the technique illegal. Although the United States has not enacted a law to ban application of the method, the federal government will not financially support any research that aims to alter inherited genes of humans.

Just Chillin'

During May 2010, the Iowa Court of Appeals ruled that a brother and sister must exhume the body of their deceased brother, Orville Richardson, so that a company could freeze his head. Orville Richardson had signed a contract with a Scottsdale, Arizona, company named Alcor Life Extension Foundation, a firm that specializes in cryonic preservation. The idea behind cryonics is that a person pays a company to freeze his or her body after death. The company will then preserve the frozen body until future science can revive that person. A cryonics client can choose a money-saving, head-only freezing option with the hope that a technique will be developed to enable a head to be grafted onto a new body.

The United States boasts at least five cryonics facilities. The preservation process requires the replacement of blood with a special antifreeze solution. Then, technicians chill the body to -320° Fahrenheit (about -196° Centigrade). The frozen body or head is stored inside a tall, stainless steel tank filled with liquid nitrogen. Pet owners have also frozen their cats and dogs for future revival.

TECHNOLOGICAL ADVANCES AND CONTROVERSIES IN LOCKSTEP

Their understanding about the roles of egg cells and sperm cells allowed scientists to focus on experiments to determine the mechanism by which parents pass traits on to their offspring. These studies revealed a new world of molecular biology populated by chromosomes, genes, and the nucleotide sequences of DNA. Studies on asexual reproduction inspired the invention of laboratory methods to clone plants and animals. Other experiments on altering genes enable scientists to produce new forms of life, such as transgenic plants and animals. Two lines of research—in vitro

For more than 35 years, cryonics specialists have struggled with a problem that occurs during freezing: the "acoustic fracturing event," or the cracking noises that signal the shattering of internal organs from extreme cold. Reviving frozen people poses a greater challenge. "To see the flaw in this system," said Michael Shermer in a 2001 *Scientific American* article, "thaw out a can of frozen strawberries. During freezing, the water within each cell expands, crystallizes, and ruptures the cell membranes. When defrosted, all the intracellular goo oozes out, turning your strawberries into runny mush. This is your brain on cryonics."

Shermer, publisher of *Skeptic* magazine, calls cryonics a "borderlands science," which is something that is not quite impossible, but is exceptionally unlikely. "The rub in exploring the borderlands," he said, "is finding that balance between being open-minded enough to accept radical new ideas but not so open-minded that your brains fall out."

Believers in cryonics stand firm in their faith that science will advance to a point where reanimation of a frozen human will become a reality. Critics of cryonics will be long dead by that time, they say, and the reanimated will enjoy the last laugh.

fertilization and gene manipulation—may one day meet and lead to the production of transgenic humans.

Technological advances often spark a need for a discussion about costs and benefits. Should scientists, for instance, genetically alter crops or livestock to suit humans? Should society allow physicians and scientists to eliminate certain inherited diseases from the human population using germline genetic modification? Would this become the first step of an ill-advised attempt to genetically "improve" human beings?

Pamela J. Hines, a senior editor at *Science* magazine, stresses the importance of an educated public to guide such decisions. "[P]ublic response to a new technology can determine what aspects of that technology are implemented, how extensively the technology is introduced, and what directions future developments on that technology may take," Hines wrote in a 2001 *AgBioForum* article. Although members of the public may not work in research labs, they are involved with scientific progress. "The availability of public funds for research, the laws restricting certain sorts of research, and the marketplace acceptance of products all affect the course of science. What is needed, therefore, is a productive discussion among scientists, educators, media, and the public at large to alleviate misunderstanding and to get at the heart of the issues, especially the controversial issues."

Glossary

asexual reproduction Reproduction that does not require the fusion of egg cell and sperm cell nuclei

base A molecule that forms part of DNA and RNA

base pair Two bases from two nucleotides, held together by weak bonds, in a double-stranded DNA or RNA molecule

chromatin A mixture of proteins and DNA

chromosome A structure in a cell that contains DNA

clone An organism that is a copy of another organism

deoxyribonucleic acid (DNA) A nucleic acid molecule that encodes genetic information and contains deoxyribose sugar

differentiate Process by which an unspecialized cell develops into a cell with specialized structures and functions

diploid A cell with two matched sets of chromosomes in its nucleus

epigenetic Changes in a gene's function that do not involve altering nucleotide sequences in DNA

fertilization Fusion of haploid egg cell and sperm cell nuclei to produce a diploid zygote

gamete An egg cell or a sperm cell

gametophyte A multicellular haploid plant

gene A nucleotide sequence that encodes a protein or a functional RNA molecule

gene expression Process in which information stored in a DNA molecule is used to make a product, such as a protein

genetic code The collection of 64 base triplets that specify 20 amino acids and the signals for stopping protein synthesis

genetic reprogramming A "reboot" of gene expression activities in the transferred nucleus of a mature, somatic cell that enables gene activities appropriate to support developmental processes in an embryo

genome The complete set of an organism's genes in the form of the collection of chromosomes found in the cell nuclei

genomic imprinting An epigenetic effect in which the parental source of a gene affects gene activity

haploid A cell with a single set of unmatched chromosomes in its nucleus

implantation Attachment of an embryo to the uterus

infertility Failure to achieve pregnancy after at least one year of frequent sex without the use of contraception

in vitro fertilization Procedure in which egg cells are removed from a woman's ovaries, mixed with sperm cells in a laboratory dish, and allowed to fertilize to form a zygote. After about five days, one or more early embryos are transferred to the future mother's uterus.

meiosis A type of cell division required to produce egg cells and sperm cells

mitosis A type of cell division that typically produces two identical daughter cells

mutation A change in the nucleotide sequence of a DNA molecule or a change in the amino acid sequence of a protein

nuclear transfer Swapping one nucleus for another to produce a clone

nucleus Intracellular structure that contains most of a cell's DNA

ovulation Release of an egg cell from an ovary

placenta Formed from maternal and fetal tissues, this organ supplies a fetus with nutrients

plasmid A ring of DNA found mostly in bacteria and capable of independent replication

polymer A large chemical made by combining smaller chemical units

protein A polymer of amino acids

recombinant DNA DNA that has been altered in the lab by the addition or deletion of nucleotide sequences

reproductive cloning Replacement of an egg cell nucleus with a somatic cell nucleus to produce an embryo that will be implanted in a surrogate mother and allowed to mature to an infant

ribonucleic acid (RNA) A nucleic acid molecule that can encode genetic information and contains ribose sugar

sexual reproduction Reproduction that requires the fusion of egg cell and sperm cell nuclei

somatic cell A cell other than an egg cell or a sperm cell

sporophyte A multicellular diploid plant

totipotent The ability of a cell to develop into a whole organism or into cells of any of its tissues

transgene A gene that is transferred to a cell, for example, in gene therapy

transgenic Describes an organism that has been genetically altered using recombinant DNA technology

vector In biotechnology, a DNA molecule that can be used to deliver a transgene

X chromosome inactivation Random inactivation of one X chromosome in the pair of X chromosomes in female mammalian cells

zygote Diploid cell produced by the fusion of haploid egg and sperm cell nuclei during fertilization

Bibliography

"The 2010 Nobel Prize in Physiology or Medicine Press Release," Nobel prize.org Web site, October 4, 2010. Available online. URL: http://nobel prize.org/nobel_prizes/medicine/laureates/2010/press.html. Accessed on January 22, 2011.

Al-Babili, Salim and Peter Beyer. "Golden Rice—Five Years on the Road—Five Years to Go?" *Trends in Plant Science* 10 (2005): 565–573.

Ali, Lorraine. "The Curious Lives of Surrogates," *Newsweek* Web site, March 29, 2008. Available online. URL: http://www.newsweek.com. Accessed on January 22, 2011.

Ally, Dilara, Kermit Ritland, and Sarah P. Otto. "Aging in a Long-Lived Clonal Tree." *PLoS Biology* 8 (2010): e1000454. Available online. URL: http://www.plosbiology.org. Accessed on November 11, 2010.

"Animal Cloning," Food and Drug Administration Web site, April 26, 2010. Available online. URL: http://www.fda.gov/AnimalVeterinary/Safety Health/AnimalCloning/default.htm. Accessed on February 11, 2011.

Antunes, M.S., K.J. Morey, J.J. Smith, K.D. Albrecht, T.A. Bowen et al. "Programmable Ligand Detection System in Plants Through a Synthetic Signal Transduction Pathway." *PLoS ONE* 6 (2011): e16292. Available online. URL: http://www.plosone.org. Accessed on February 17, 2011.

"Assisted Reproduction Technology Has No Effect on Birth Process or Baby's Outcome," Norwegian University of Science and Technology Web site, March 1, 2010. Available online. URL: http://www.ntnu.edu. Accessed on November 11, 2010.

"Background: Cloned and Genetically Modified Animals," Center for Genetics and Society Web site, April 14, 2005. Available online. URL: http://www.geneticsandsociety.org. Accessed on February 9, 2011.

"Biotech Crops Surge over 1 Billion Hectares," ISAAA Web site, February 22, 2011. Available online. URL: http://www.isaaa.org. Accessed on February 25, 2011.

Booth, Warren, Daniel H. Johnson, Sharon Moore, Coby Schal, and Edward L. Vargo. "Evidence for Viable, Non-clonal But Fatherless Boa Constrictors." Biology Letters, November 3, 2010. Available online. URL: http://rsbl.royalsocietypublishing.org. Accessed on January 15, 2011.

Boyd, Jade. "Biomedical Breakthrough: Blood Vessels for Lab-grown Tissues," Rice University Web site, January 12, 2011. Available online. URL: http://www.media.rice.edu. Accessed on January 28, 2011.

Bruder C.E., A. Piotrowski, A.A. Gijsbers, R. Andersson, S. Erickson et al. "Phenotypically Concordant and Discordant Monozygotic Twins Display Different DNA Copy-number-variation Profiles. *The American Journal of Human Genetics* 82 (2008): 763–771.

Brus, Brian. "Oklahoma Farmer Finds Savings in Cloning." *The Journal Record* (Oklahoma City), November 23, 2009.

Capanna, Ernesto. "Lazzaro Spallanzani: At the Roots of Modern Biology." *Journal of Experimental Zoology* 285 (1999): 178–196.

Chang, Kenneth. "Scientist in Clone Tests Says Hoax is Possible." *The New York Times*, January 7, 2003.

Choi, Charles Q. "First Extinct-Animal Clone Created," National Geographic Web site, February 10, 2009. Available online. URL: http://news.nationalgeographic.com. Accessed on February 8, 2011.

Clark, John and Bruce Whitelaw. "A Future for Transgenic Livestock." *Nature Reviews Genetics* 4 (2003): 825–833.

"Cloning Myths," University of Utah Web site, 2011. Available online. URL: http://learn.genetics.utah.edu. Accessed on February 23, 2011.

Connor, Steve. "GM Mosquitoes Deployed to Control Asia's Dengue Fever." *The Independent* (London), January 27, 2011.

Cooper, Geoffrey M. and Robert E. Hausman. *The Cell: A Molecular Approach*. 5th ed. Washington, D.C.: ASM Press, 2009.

Cormick, Craig. "Cloning Goes to the Movies." *História, Ciências, Saúde–Manguinhos* 13 (October 2006): 181–212.

Crumb, Michael J. "Iowa Court: Exhume Body So Head Can Be Frozen," ABC News Web site, May 14, 2010. Available online. URL: http://abcnews.go.com. Accessed on February 17, 2011.

De Cozar, Tara. "Turning Back the Clock to Save the Bramley Apple," The University of Nottingham Web Site, March 23, 2009. Available online. URL: http://www.nottingham.ac.uk. Accessed on January 31, 2011.

"The Emperor's New Clones." *Nature Biotechnology* 25 (January 2007): 1.

"Evolution of Self-Fertilization," Science Daily Web site, November 10, 2010. Available online. URL: http://www.sciencedaily.com. Accessed on February 3, 2011.

Francuch, Paul. "Nightshades' Mating Habits Strike Uneasy Evolutionary Balance," UIC News Bureau Web site, October 21, 2010. Available online. URL: www.news.uic.edu. Accessed on February 3, 2011.

Garcia, Jairo E. "In Vitro Fertilization," eMedicineHealth Web site, August 10, 2005. Available online. URL: http://www.emedicinehealth.com. Accessed on November 12, 2010.

Gilbert, Scott F. *Developmental Biology*. 9th ed. Sunderland, Mass: Sinauer Associates, Inc., 2010.

"GM Chickens That Don't Transmit Bird Flu Developed," University of Cambridge Web site, January 13, 2011. Available online. URL: http://www.admin.cam.ac.uk. Accessed on February 16, 2011.

"Golden Rice: Sustainable Biofortification for the Poor Rural Population," Golden Rice Project Web site, 2007. Available online. URL: http://www.goldenrice.org. Accessed on February 13, 2011.

Hanna, Kathi E. "Germline Gene Transfer," National Human Genome Research Institute Web site, March 2006. Available online. URL: http://www.genome.gov/10004764. Accessed on February 16, 2011.

Hartwell, Leland H., Leroy Hood, Michael L. Goldberg, Ann E. Reynolds, Lee M. Silver et al. *Genetics: From Genes to Genomes*. 3rd ed. New York: McGraw-Hill, 2008.

Hawthorne, Lou. "Six Reasons We're No Longer Cloning Dogs." BioArts International Web site, September 10, 2009. Available online. URL: http://www.bioarts.com. Accessed on February 7, 2011.

Heyman, Yvan, Xavier Vignon, Patrick Chesné, Daniel Le Bourhis, Jacques Marchal et al. "Cloning in Cattle: From Embryo Splitting to Somatic Nuclear Transfer." *Reproduction Nutrition Développement* 38 (1998): 595–603.

Hickman, Cleveland P. Jr., Larry S. Roberts, Allan Larson, Helen L'Anson, and David J. Eisenhour. *Integrated Principles of Zoology*. 13th ed. New York: McGraw-Hill, 2006.

Hines, Pamela J. "The Dynamics of Scientific Controversies." *AgBioForum* 4 (2001): 186–193.

"How Aspens Grow," U.S. Forest Service Web site, October 13, 2010. Available online. URL: http://www.fs.fed.us/wildflowers/communities/aspen/grow.shtml. Accessed on February 2, 2011.

Hughes, David P., Torsten Wappler, and Conrad C. Labandeira. "Ancient Death-grip Leaf Scars Reveal Ant-fungal Parasitism." *Biology Letters* 7 (2011): 67–70.

"Improving Clinical Use of Stem Cells to Repair Heart Damage," Science-Daily Web site, July 16, 2010. Available online. URL: http://www.science daily.com. Accessed on November 14, 2010.

"Infertility," Mayo Clinic Web site, June 27, 2009. Available online. URL: http://www.mayoclinic.com. Accessed on January 22, 2011.

Johnson, Brian. "Genetically Modified Crops and Other Organisms: Implications for Agricultural Sustainability and Biodiversity." In *Agricultural Biotechnology and the Poor*. G. J. Persley and M. M. Lantin, eds., Washington, D.C.: The World Bank, 1999, 131–138.

Johnson, Kirk. "Plants That Earn Their Keep." *The New York Times*, January 26, 2011.

Jonsson, Patrik. "Nobel Prize for Robert Edwards: The Controversies Behind IVF," *Christian Science Monitor* Web site, October 4, 2010. Available online. URL: http://www.csmonitor.com. Accessed on November 11, 2011.

Karp, Gerald. *Cell and Molecular Biology*. 6th ed. New York: John Wiley & Sons, Inc., 2010.

Klotzko, Arlene Judith (ed.) *The Cloning Sourcebook*. New York: Oxford University Press, 2001.

Kurpinski, Kyle and Terry D. Johnson. *How to Defeat Your Own Clone*. New York: Bantam Books, 2010.

"Leading Cloning Experts Challenge Clonaid To Prove Claim," Science Daily Web site, January 7, 2003. Available online. URL: http://www.science daily.com. Accessed on February 10, 2011.

Lechevalier, Hubert. "Louis Joblot and His Microscopes." *Bacteriological Reviews* 40 (1976): 241–258.

Levine, Russell and Chris Evers. "The Slow Death of Spontaneous Generation (1668-1859)," Access Excellence Web site. Available online. URL: http://www.accessexcellence.org. Accessed on February 21, 2011.

Long, John A. "Dawn of the Deed." *Scientific American* 304 (January 2011): 35–39.

Masterson, Ursula Owre. "Cloning pets: In search of Fluffy 2.0," msnbc.com Web site, 2011. Available online. URL: http://www.msnbc.msn.com. Accessed on February 9, 2011.

Meinke, Sue A. "Surrogate Motherhood: Ethical and Legal Issues," Bioethics Research Library at Georgetown University Web site, 1988. Available online. URL: http://bioethics.georgetown.edu. Accessed on January 22, 2011.

Milton, Joseph. "GM Maize Offers Windfall For Conventional Farms." *Nature* News Web site, October 7, 2010. Available online. URL: http://www.nature.com. Accessed on February 16, 2011.

Moore, Tom and Melanie Ball. "Kaguya, the First Parthenogenetic Mammal—Engineering Triumph or Lottery Winner?" *Reproduction* 128 (2004): 1–3.

Mott, Maryann. "Cat Cloning Offered to Pet Owners," National Geographic Web site, March 25, 2004. Available online. URL: http://news.nationalgeographic.com. Accessed on February 6, 2011.

Mott, Maryann. "Dog Cloned by South Korean Scientists," National Geographic Web site, August 3, 2005. Available online. URL: http://news.nationalgeographic.com. Accessed on February 9, 2011.

National Academy of Sciences, National Academy of Engineering, Institute of Medicine, National Research Council. *Scientific and Medical Aspects of Human Reproductive Cloning*. Washington, D.C.: National Academy Press, 2002.

Norman H.D., T.J. Lawlor, J.R. Wright, and R.L. Powell. "Performance of Holstein Clones in the United States." *Journal of Dairy Science* 87 (2004): 729–738.

O'Hanlon, Larry. "Cloning Has Terrible Trade-offs," *Discovery* News Web site, August 18, 2010. Available online. URL: http://news.discovery.com. Accessed on January 31, 2011.

Osgood, Marcy, P. "X-Chromosome Inactivation: The Case of the Calico Cat." *American Journal of Pharmaceutical Education* 58 (1994): 204–205.

Pinto-Correia, Clara. *The Ovary of Eve*. Chicago: The University of Chicago Press, 1997.

Pollack, Andrew. "F.D.A. Approves Drug From Gene-Altered Goats." *The New York Times*, February 6, 2009.

"A Primer on Cloning and Its Use in Livestock Operations," U.S. FDA Web site, October 28, 2009. Available online. URL: http://www.fda.gov/Animal Veterinary/SafetyHealth/AnimalCloning/ucm055513.htm. Accessed on February 7, 2011.

Prince of Wales. "The Seeds of Disaster." *The Daily Telegraph* (London), June 7, 1998.

Reece, Jane B., Lisa A. Urry, Michael L. Cain, Steven A. Wasserman, Peter V. Minorsky et al. *Campbell Biology*. 9th ed. San Francisco: Pearson/Benjamin Cummings, 2011.

Ryan, Kenneth J. and C. George Ray, eds. *Sherris Medical Microbiology*. 5th ed. New York: McGraw-Hill, 2010.

Sachs, David H. and Cesare Galli. "Genetic Manipulation in Pigs." *Current Opinion in Organ Transplantation* 14 (2009): 148–153.

Scott, Elizabeth S. "Surrogacy and the Politics of Commodification." *Law and Contemporary Problems* 72 (2009): 109–146.

Shermer, Michael. "Nano Nonsense and Cryonics." *Scientific American* 285 (2001): 29.

"Son of Frankenfood?" *The Economist* (London) 386, January 19, 2008: 62.

Stein, Rob. "Developer of In Vitro Fertilization Wins Nobel." *The Washington Post* (October 5, 2010).

Storck, Susan. "In Vitro Fertilization (IVF)," MedlinePlus Web site, February 10, 2010. Available online. URL: http://www.nlm.nih.gov/medline plus/ency/article/007279.htm. Accessed on January 22, 2011.

"Study Shows Promise That Heart Damage in Children Could be Repaired by Using Stem Cells From Patient's Own Heart," Children's Memorial Hospital Web site, January 27, 2011. Available online. URL: http://www .childrensmemorial.org. Accessed on January 28, 2011.

Thuan, Nguyen Van, Satoshi Kishigami, and Teruhiko Wakayama. "How to Improve the Success Rate of Mouse Cloning Technology." *Journal of Reproduction and Development* 56 (2010): 20–30.

Trivedi, Bijal P. "Scientists Clone First Endangered Species: a Wild Sheep," National Geographic Web site, October 29, 2001. Available online. URL: http://news.nationalgeographic.com. Accessed on February 7, 2011.

"Veterinary Researchers Achieve Cloning First," Texas A&M News and Information Services Web site, June 11, 2010. Available online. URL: http://tamunews.tamu.edu. Accessed on February 8, 2011.

Weiss, Rick. "Cloning a Previous Hoax?" *The Washington Post*, December 31, 2002.

Wiegand, Susan. "William Harvey (1578–1657)," Access Excellence Web site. Available online. URL: http://www.accessexcellence.org/RC/AB/BC/William_Harvey.php. Accessed on February 22, 2011.

Wilmsen, Emily Narvaes. "Colorado State University Biologist Produces Plant Sentinels that Detect Environmental Contaminants, Explosives," Colorado State University Web site, January 26, 2011. Available online. URL: http://www.news.colostate.edu. Accessed on February 16, 2011.

Wilson, John. "Stanford University School of Medicine and the Predecessor Schools : An Historical Perspective," Lane Medical Library Web site, April 12, 2000. Available online. URL: http://elane.stanford.edu/wilson/index.html. Accessed on February 21, 2011.

Witt, Howard. "The Cold, Hard Facts on Cryonics." *Chicago Tribune*, August 23, 2005.

Wolpert, Lewis, Cheryll Tickle, Thomas Jessell, Peter Lawrence, Elliot Meyerowitz et al. *Principles of Development.* 4th ed. New York: Oxford University Press, 2011.

"Zombie Ants Controlled by Fungus." LiveScience Web site, August 12, 2009. Available online. URL: http://www.livescience.com. Accessed on January 10, 2011.

Further Resources

Books

Ballard, Carol. *Understanding Reproduction*. New York: Rosen Publishing Group, 2010.

Boleyn-Fitzgerald, Miriam. *Beginning Life*. New York: Chelsea House, 2010.

Farndon, John. *From DNA to GM Wheat: Discovering Genetic Modification of Food*. Portsmouth, N.H.: Heinemann Educational Books, 2008.

Hodge, Russ. *Human Genetics*. New York: Chelsea House, 2010.

Hopkins, William G. *Plant Biotechnology*. New York: Chelsea House, 2006.

Judson, Karen. *Genetic Engineering: Debating the Benefits and Concerns*. Berkeley Heights, N.J.: Enslow Publishers, Inc., 2001.

Krohmer, Randolph. *The Reproductive System*. New York: Chelsea House, 2009.

Panno, Joseph. *Animal Cloning*. New York: Chelsea House, 2010.

Simpson, Kathleen. *National Geographic Investigates: Genetics: From DNA to Designer Dogs*. Washington, D.C.: National Geographic Children's Books, 2008.

Spilsbury, Richard. *Reproduction and Genetics*. Chicago: Heinemann Library, 2008.

Web sites

Access Excellence @ the National Health Museum
http://www.accessexcellence.org
> *The National Health Museum offers general information and images about agricultural biotechnology, an overview of the history of biotechnology, and insights into many aspects of genetic science.*

Animal Cloning

http://www.fda.gov/AnimalVeterinary/SafetyHealth/Animal
Cloning/default.htm

The U.S. Food and Drug Administration provides basic information about cloning—with an emphasis on livestock cloning. The agency also explains its views on the safety of food produced by the offspring of livestock clones.

Genetic Science Learning Center

http://learn.genetics.utah.edu/content/tech/cloning

The University of Utah provides information on cloning science. Visitors can use the Web site's "Click and Clone" function to experience the technique of cloning a mouse.

Human Embryology Animations

http://www.indiana.edu/~anat550/embryo_main/index.html

Indiana University offers animated tutorials on topics in human embryology, including cardiovascular embryology, development of limbs and head, and embryology of the gastrointestinal tract.

ReproductiveFacts.org

http://www.reproductivefacts.org

Offered by the American Society for Reproductive Medicine, this Web site explores topics in human reproduction, such as infertility, in vitro fertilization, and contraception.

Science Daily

http://www.sciencedaily.com/

The Science Daily website is a comprehensive source for news about science research, including news about developments in genetic engineering, cloning, and reproduction science.

Transgenic Crops

http://cls.casa.colostate.edu/transgeniccrops/index.html

The Department of Soil and Crop Sciences at Colorado State University offers basic information on the production of transgenic crops and a history of plant breeding.

Picture Credits

Page

Index

About the Author

Phill Jones earned a Ph.D. in physiology and pharmacology from the University of California at San Diego, where he specialized in reproductive medicine. After completing postdoctoral training at Stanford University School of Medicine, he joined the Department of Biochemistry at the University of Kentucky Medical Center as an assistant professor. Here, he taught courses in molecular biology and medicine, and researched aspects of gene expression. He later earned a JD at the University of Kentucky College of Law and worked for 10 years as a patent attorney, specializing in biological, chemical, and medical inventions. Dr. Jones is now a full-time writer. His articles have appeared in *Today's Science on File, The World Almanac and Book of Facts, History Magazine, Forensic Magazine, Encyclopedia of Forensic Science, The Science of Michael Crichton, Forensic Nurse Magazine, Nature Biotechnology, Information Systems for Biotechnology News Report, Law and Order Magazine, PharmaTechnology Magazine,* and educational testing publications. His books, *Sickle Cell Disease* (2008), *The Genetic Code* (2010), and *Kingdoms of Life* (2011) were published by Chelsea House. For more than six years, he has taught his online course in forensic science for writers. His science fiction/mystery novella, *Thin Ice* (2010), and numerous short stories have also seen publication.